# Progressive
# GUITAR METHOD
# Book 1
## Tablature Version

### by
### Gary Turner & Brenton White

**Visit our Website**
**www.learntoplaymusic.com**

*The Progressive Series of Music Instruction Books, CDs, and DVDs*

# CONTENTS

# INTRODUCTION

**THE PROGRESSIVE GUITAR METHOD** is a series of books designed to take the Guitar student from a beginner level through to a professional standard of playing. All books are carefully graded, lesson by lesson methods which assume no prior knowledge on your behalf. Within the series all styles and techniques of guitar playing are covered, including reading music, playing chords and rhythms, lead guitar and fingerpicking.

**PROGRESSIVE GUITAR METHOD BOOK 1: BEGINNER** assumes you have no prior knowledge of music or playing the guitar. **PROGRESSIVE GUITAR METHOD BOOK 1: BEGINNER** will teach you the notes on each of the six strings, together with basic elements of music theory including time signatures, note values, sharps, flats and the chromatic scale. This theory is essential to help you understand the guitar and can be applied to solve practical problems, hence speeding up your progress. This book also has special sections on tuning, how to read sheet music and a chord chart. Upon its completion you will have a solid understanding of guitar. All guitarists should know all of the information in this book. In conjunction with this book you can use other books in the progressive series to learn about tablature reading, lead guitar playing, fingerpicking, bar chords, slide and classical guitar styles as well as music theory and different styles such as Rock, Blues, Country, Jazz, Metal and Funk.

The best and fastest way to learn is to use these books in conjunction with:
1.   Buying sheet music and song books of your favourite recording artists and learning to play their songs.
2.   Practicing and playing with other musicians. You will be surprised how good a basic drums/bass/guitar combination can sound even when playing easy music.
3.   Learning by listening to your favourite CDs.

Also in the early stages it is helpful to have the guidance of an experienced teacher. This will also help you keep to a schedule and obtain weekly goals.

It is recommended that you should also study the Progressive Guitar Method Book 1: Supplement which contains 70 more songs and 8 more lessons containing information on major scales, keys, triplets, $\frac{6}{8}$ time, sixteenth notes and syncopation.

# APPROACH TO PRACTICE

It is important to have a correct approach to practice. You will benefit more from several short practices (e.g. 15-30 minutes per day) than one or two long sessions per week. This is especially so in the early stages, because of the basic nature of the material being studied. In a practice session you should divide your time evenly between the study of new material and the revision of past work. It is a common mistake for semi-advanced students to practice only the pieces they can already play well. Although this is more enjoyable, it is not a very satisfactory method of practice. You should also try to correct mistakes and experiment with new ideas. It is the author's belief that an experienced teacher will be an invaluable aid to your progress.

4

# OTHER TITLES IN THIS SERIES

There is now a whole series of *Progressive Guitar Method* Books which covers all aspeccts of guitar playing. While you are studying this book, you will find *Guitar Method Book 1 Supplement* and *Guitar Method: Theory* particularly useful. On completion of this book, you will be ready to study specific types of guitar playing such as Rhythm and Lead. Shown below are the rest of the Guitar Method series, along with a brief description of each title.

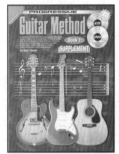

### Guitar Method
### Book 1: Supplement

A collection of over 70 well known songs with chord symbols which can be used along or in conjunction with Progressive Guitar Method Book 1. Contains 8 more lessons on major scales, keys, triplets, 6/8 time, 16th notes, syncopation and swing rhythms.

### Guitar Method
### Rhythm

Introduces all the important open chord shapes for major, minor, seventh, sixth, major seventh, minor seventh, suspended, diminished and augmented chords. Learn to play over 50 chord progressions, including 12 Bar Blues and Turnaround progressions.

### Guitar Method
### Lead

Covers scales and patterns over the entire fretboard so that you can improvise against major, minor, and Blues progressions in any key. Learn the licks and techniques used by all lead guitarists such as hammer-ons, slides, bending, vibrato, and more.

### Guitar Method
### Fingerpicking

Introduces right hand fingerpicking patterns that can be used as an accompaniment to any chord, chord progression or song. Covers alternate thumb, arpeggio and constant bass style as used in Rock, Pop, Folk, Country, Blues Ragtime and Classical music.

### Guitar Method
### Chords

Contains the most useful open, Bar and Jazz chord shapes of the most used chord types with chord progressions to practice and play along with. Includes sections on tuning, how to read sheet music, transposing, as well as an easy chord table, formula and symbol chart.

### Guitar Method
### Bar Chords

Introduces the most useful Bar, Rock and Jazz chord shapes used by all Rock/Pop/Country and Blues guitarist. Includes major, minor, seventh, sixth, major seventh, etc. Suggested rhythm patterns including percussive strums, dampening and others are also covered.

### Guitar Method
### Book 2

A comprehensive, lesson by lesson method covering the most important keys and scales for guitar, with special emphasis on bass note picking, bass note runs, hammer-ons etc. Featuring chordal arrangements of well known Rock, Blues, Folk and Traditional songs.

### Guitar Method
### Theory Book 1

A comprehensive, introduction to music theory as it applies to the guitar. Covers reading traditional music, rhythm notation and tablature, along with learning the notes on the fretboard, how to construct chords and scales, transposition, musical terms and playing in all keys.

For more information about the *Progressive Guitar Method* series as well as the general *Progressive* series, contact:

LTP Publishing
email: info@learntoplaymusic.com
or visit our website;
**www.learntoplaymusic.com**

# USING THE COMPACT DISC

It is recommended that you have a copy of the accompanying compact disc that includes all the examples in this book. The book shows you where to put your fingers and what technique to use and the recording lets you hear how each example should sound. Practice the examples slowly at first, gradually increasing tempo. Once you are confident you can play the example evenly without stopping the beat, try playing along with the recording. You will hear a drum beat at the beginning of each example, to lead you into the example and to help you keep time. To play along with the CD your guitar must be in tune with it (see page 58). If you have tuned using an electronic tuner (see below) your guitar will already be in tune with the CD. A small diagram of a compact disc with a number as shown below indicates a recorded example.

 **12** ←— CD Track Number

# ELECTRONIC TUNER

The easiest and most accurate way to tune your guitar is by using an **electronic tuner**. An electronic tuner allows you to tune each string individually to the tuner, by indicating whether the notes are sharp (too high) or flat (too low). If you have an electric guitar you can plug it directly in to the tuner. If you have an acoustic guitar the tuner will have an inbuilt microphone. There are several types of electronic guitar tuners but

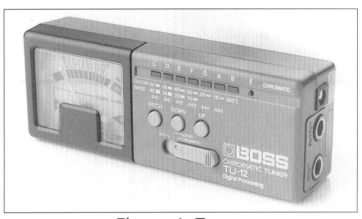

*Electronic Tuner*

most are relatively inexpensive and simple to operate. Tuning using other methods is difficult for beginning guitarists and it takes many months to master, so we recommend you purchase an electronic tuner, particularly if you do not have a guitar teacher or a friend who can tune it for you. Also if your guitar is way out of tune you can always take it to your local music store so they can tune it for you. Once a guitar has been tuned correctly it should only need minor adjustments before each practice session. To learn to tune the guitar using other methods see page 58.

# TUNING YOUR GUITAR TO THE CD

Before you commence each lesson or practice session you will need to tune your guitar. If your guitar is out of tune everything you play will sound incorrect even though you are holding the correct notes. On the accompanying CD the **first six tracks** correspond to the **six strings of the guitar**. For a complete description of how to tune your guitar, see page 58.

**1. 6th String**
**E Note** (Thickest string)

**2. 5th String**
**A Note**

**3. 4th String**
**D Note**

**4. 3rd String**
**G Note**

**5. 2nd String**
**B Note**

**6. 1st String**
**E Note** (Thinnest string)

# ACOUSTIC GUITARS

### Classical Guitar
#### (Nylon Strings)

### Steel String Acoustic

The **classical guitar** has nylon strings and a wider neck than the other types of guitar. It is most commonly used for playing Classical, Flamenco and Fingerstyles. Generally it is much cheaper than other types of guitar and is recommended for beginning guitarists.

The **steel string acoustic** has steel strings and is most commonly played by strumming or fingerpicking groups of notes called chords. This is the type of acoustic guitar you will hear in most modern styles of music e.g. Top 40 Rock and Pop music.

# ELECTRIC GUITARS

Electric guitars have **pick-ups** (a type of inbuilt microphone) and need to be played into an **amplifier** (amp) to be heard.

The **solid body electric** is commonly used in Metal, Rock, Blues and Pop Music. Famous solid body guitars are the **Gibson Les Paul** and the **Fender Stratocaster**.

The **hollow body electric** (semi acoustic) is most commonly used in Jazz and Blues music.

Acoustic guitars can be amplified by using a microphone placed near the sound hole or by placing a portable pick-up on the body of the guitar e.g. for performances at large venues where the acoustic guitar needs amplification to be heard.

# ELECTRIC GUITARS
## *(PLAYED THROUGH AN AMPLIFIER)*

### *Solid Body Electric*      *Hollow Body Electric*
### *(semi acoustic)*

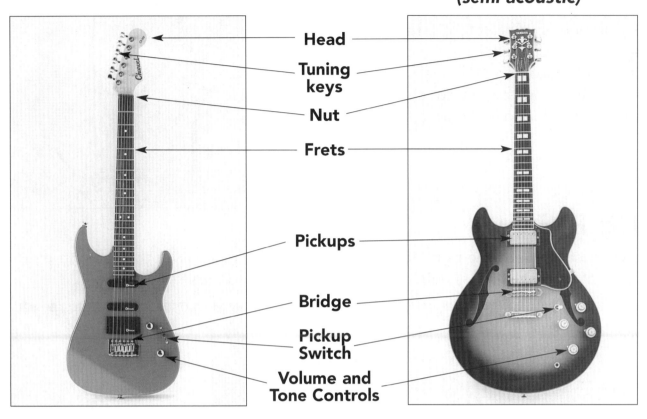

- Head
- Tuning keys
- Nut
- Frets
- Pickups
- Bridge
- Pickup Switch
- Volume and Tone Controls

# AMPLIFIERS
## *Combo*
### *(combined amp and speaker)*

## *Stack*
### *(separate amp head and speaker)*

# STRINGS

It is important to have the correct set of strings fitted to your guitar, especially if you are a beginner. Until you build enough strength in your hands to fret the chords cleanly, light gauge or low tension strings are recommended. A reputable music store which sells guitar strings should be able to assist with this. Do not put steel strings on a classical guitar or it will damage the neck of the guitar. It is important to change your strings regularly, as old strings go out of tune easily and are more difficult to keep in tune.

# SEATING

Before you commence playing, a comfortable seating position is required. Most modern guitarists prefer to sit with their right leg raised, (as shown in the photo) or by placing your right foot on a footstool. The guitar should be close to the body, and in a vertical position. The main aim is for comfort and easy access to the guitar. A music stand will also be helpful.

# THE PICK

The contact between the right hand and the strings is made with the use of a pick (also called a plectrum), which is held between the thumb and index finger.

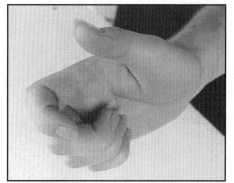

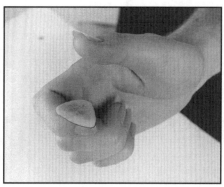

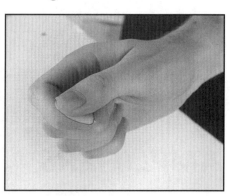

1. Index finger curved.

2. Pick placed on first joint of index finger with its point about ¼ inch (6mm) past the finger-tip.

3. Thumb clamps down, holding the pick in place.

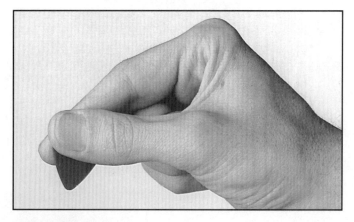

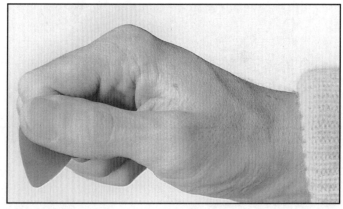

**INCORRECT**
**First finger not curved.**

**INCORRECT**
**Pick incorrectly placed on second joint of index finger.**

Picks are usually made of plastic and come in a variety of different shapes and thicknesses. You should experiment until you find one which you feel comfortable with. Use the tip of the pick to play the string.

# RIGHT ARM POSITION

The correct position for the right arm is illustrated in **Photo A** below. Notice that the fore-arm rests on the upper edge of the guitar, just below the elbow. Be careful not to have the elbow hanging over the face of the guitar or your hand too far along the fretboard (**Photo B**).

**Photo A: CORRECT**

**Photo B: INCORRECT**

## THE LEFT HAND

The left hand fingers are numbered as such:

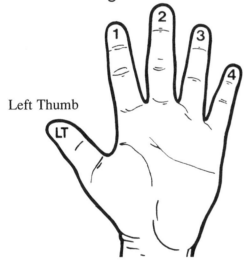

## LEFT HAND PLACEMENT

Your fingers should be **on their tips** and placed just **behind** the frets (not on top of them).

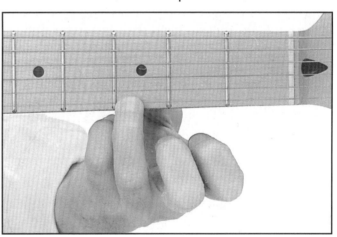

Be careful not to allow the thumb to hang too far over the top of the neck (**Photo C**), or to let it run parallel along the back of the neck (**Photo D**).

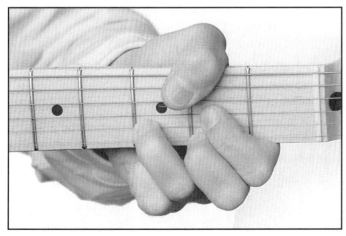

**Photo C: INCORRECT**

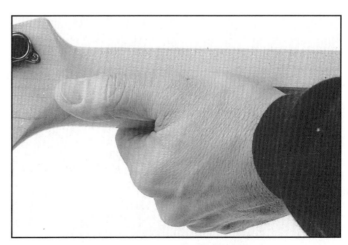

**Photo D: INCORRECT**

# HOW TO READ MUSIC

There are two methods used to write guitar music. First is the **traditional music notation** method (using music notes, ♩) and second is **tablature.** Both are used in this book but you need only use one of these methods. Most guitarists find Tablature easier to read, however, it is very worthwhile to learn to read traditional music notation as well. Nearly all sheet music you buy in a store is written in traditional notation.

## TABLATURE

Tablature is a method of indicating the position of notes on the fretboard. There are six "tab" lines each representing one of the six strings of the guitar. Study the following diagram.

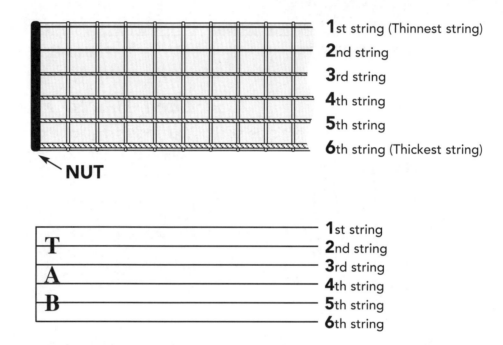

When a number is placed on one of the lines, it indicates the fret location of a note e.g.

This indicates the open 3rd string (a G note).

This indicates the 3rd fret of the 5th string (a C note).

This indicates the 1st fret of the 1st string (an F note).

# THE RUDIMENTS OF MUSIC

The musical alphabet consists of 7 letters:

A B C D E F G

Music is written on a **staff**, which consists of 5 parallel lines between which there are 4 spaces.

**MUSIC STAFF**

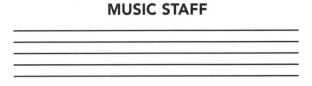

**The treble or 'G' clef** is placed at the beginning of each staff line. This clef indicates the position of the note G. (It is an old fashioned method of writing the letter G, with the centre of the clef being written on the second staff line.)

The other lines and spaces on the staff are named as such:

Extra notes can be added by the use of short lines, called **leger lines**.

When a note is placed on the staff its head indicates its position, e.g.:

**This is a G note**

**This is a C note**

When the note head is below the middle staff line the stem points upward and when the head is above the middle line the stem points downward. A note placed on the middle line (**B**) can have its stem pointing either up or down.

**Bar lines** are drawn across the staff, which divides the music into sections called **bars** or **measures**. A **double bar line** signifies either the end of the music, or the end of an important section of it.

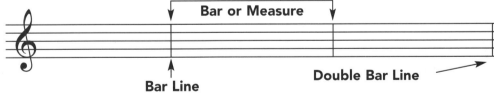

# NOTE VALUES

The table below sets out the most common notes used in music and their respective time values (i.e. length of time held). For each note value there is an equivalent rest, which indicates a period of silence.

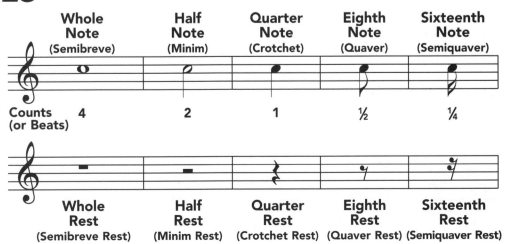

| | Whole Note (Semibreve) | Half Note (Minim) | Quarter Note (Crotchet) | Eighth Note (Quaver) | Sixteenth Note (Semiquaver) |
|---|---|---|---|---|---|
| Counts (or Beats) | 4 | 2 | 1 | ½ | ¼ |
| | Whole Rest (Semibreve Rest) | Half Rest (Minim Rest) | Quarter Rest (Crotchet Rest) | Eighth Rest (Quaver Rest) | Sixteenth Rest (Semiquaver Rest) |

| | | |
|---|---|---|
| **Dotted half note** | 𝅗𝅥· | (2 + 1) = 3 counts |
| **Dotted quarter note** | ♩· | (1 + ½) = 1½ counts |
| **Dotted whole note** | 𝅝· | (4 + 2) = 6 counts |

A **tie** is a curved line joining two or more notes of the same pitch, where the second note(s) **is note played** but its time value is added to that of the first note. Here are two examples:

In both of these examples only the first note is played.

# TIME SIGNATURES

At the beginning of each piece of music, after the treble clef, is the **time signature**.

**Time Signature**
**(pronounced Four Four time)**

**4** – this indicates 4 beats per bar.

**4** – this indicates that each beat is worth a quarter note (crotchet).

The time signature indicates the number of beats per bar (the top number) and the type of note receiving one beat (the bottom number). For example:

Thus in $\frac{4}{4}$ time there must be the equivalent of 4 quarter note beats per bar, e.g.

$\frac{4}{4}$ is the most common time signature and is sometimes represented by this symbol called **common time**.

**common time**

The other time signature used in this book is Three Four Time written $\frac{3}{4}$.
$\frac{3}{4}$ indicates 3 quarter note beats per bar, e.g.

# LESSON ONE

## FIRST STRING NOTES

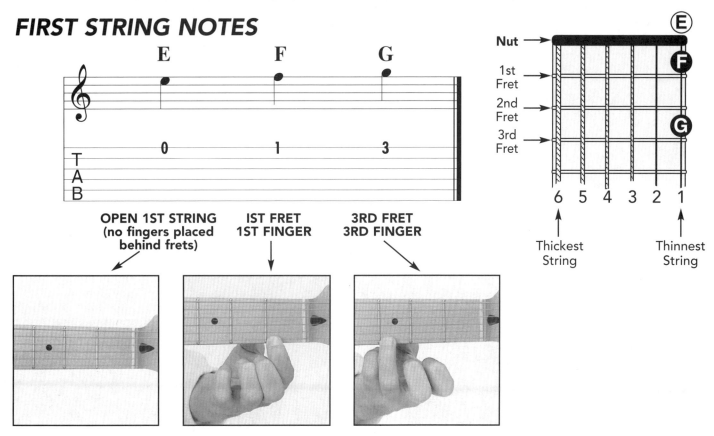

OPEN 1ST STRING
(no fingers placed
behind frets)

IST FRET
1ST FINGER

3RD FRET
3RD FINGER

Place your fingers **on their tips**, immediately **behind** the frets and **press** hard to avoid buzzing or deadened notes.

The following examples use **quarter notes** (or crotchets) ♩, worth one count each **(see page 11)**. Use a **downward** pick motion ⋁. This will apply to all examples and songs until otherwise instructed.

**7**

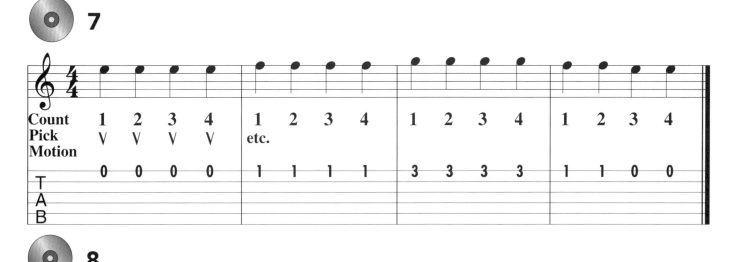

**8**

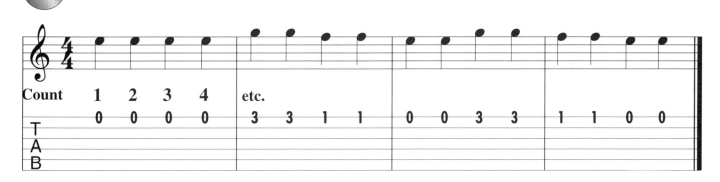

**9**

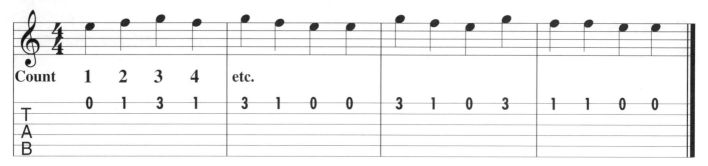

## RIGHT HAND SUPPORT

It is necessary for the right hand to be supported on the guitar by either (**1**) the palm resting against the bridge or (**2**) resting fingers on the pick guard. This will feel more comfortable and aid in the development of speed by encouraging a down/up movement rather than an in/out movement of the pick.

**(1) Palm support on bridge**

**(2) Finger support on pick guard**

## PICK TECHNIQUE

You should not let the pick 'dig in' to the strings, but rather play using only its tip.

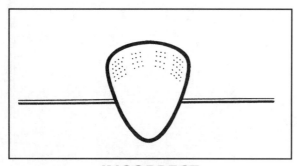

**INCORRECT**

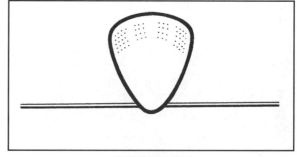

**CORRECT**

## TROUBLESHOOTING

- Play **slowly** and **evenly. Do not** attempt to go fast as accuracy is more important at this level.
- Place your fingers directly **behind** the frets (**as shown in the photos**) and **on their tips.**
- **Count** (in groups of four) in your head or out loud as you play.
- Be sure to support your wrist and use correct pick technique.

# LESSON TWO

## SECOND STRING NOTES

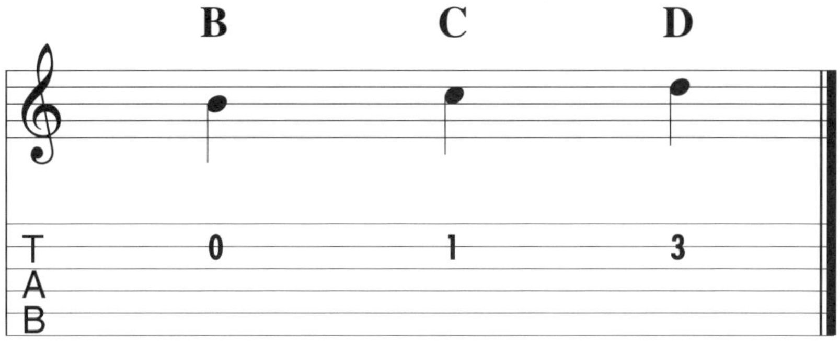
B
C
D
T
A
B
0
1
3

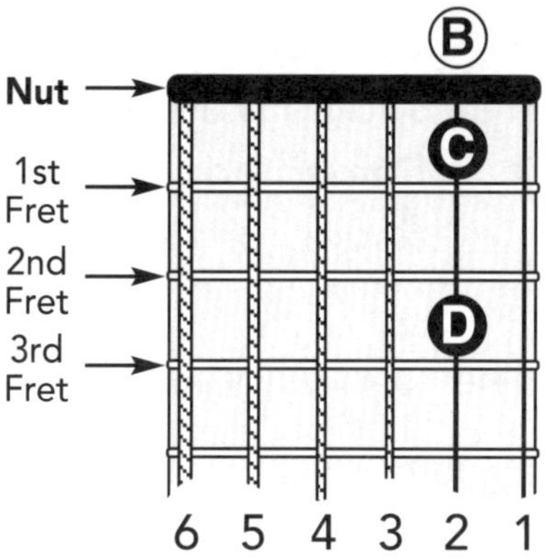
Nut
1st Fret
2nd Fret
3rd Fret
B
C
D
6 5 4 3 2 1

OPEN 2ND STRING

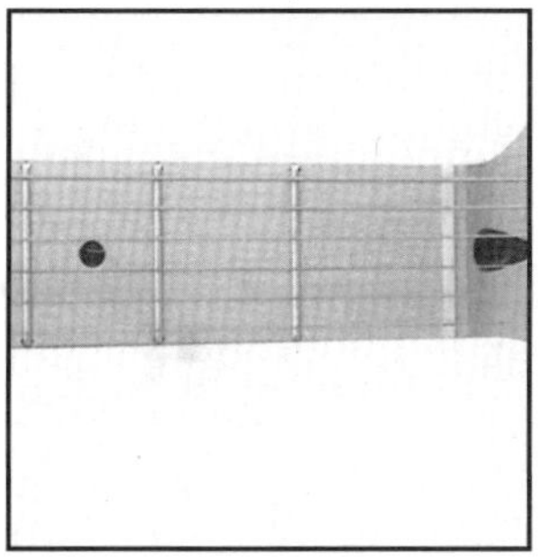

IST FRET
1ST FINGER

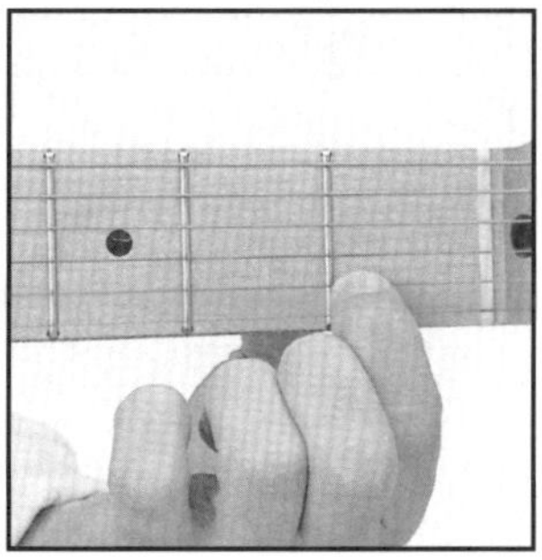

3RD FRET
3RD FINGER

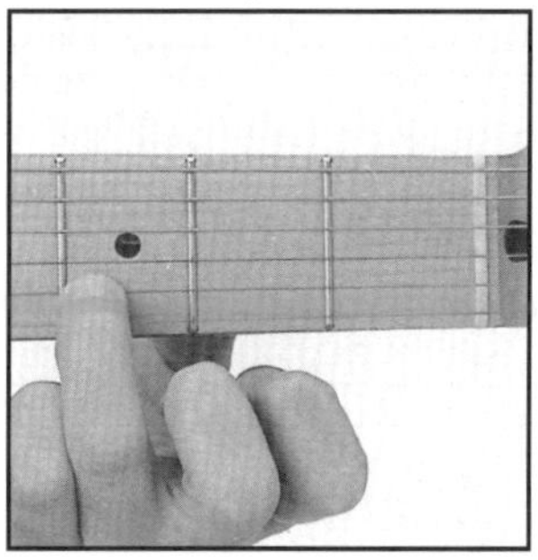

**Ex. 10** introduces the **half-note** (or minim) 𝅗𝅥, which is worth two counts. In bar 8 the half notes are played on the first and third beats, as indicated by the count. This exercise is 8 bars long. Bar numbers are the small numbers written below the staff.

**10**

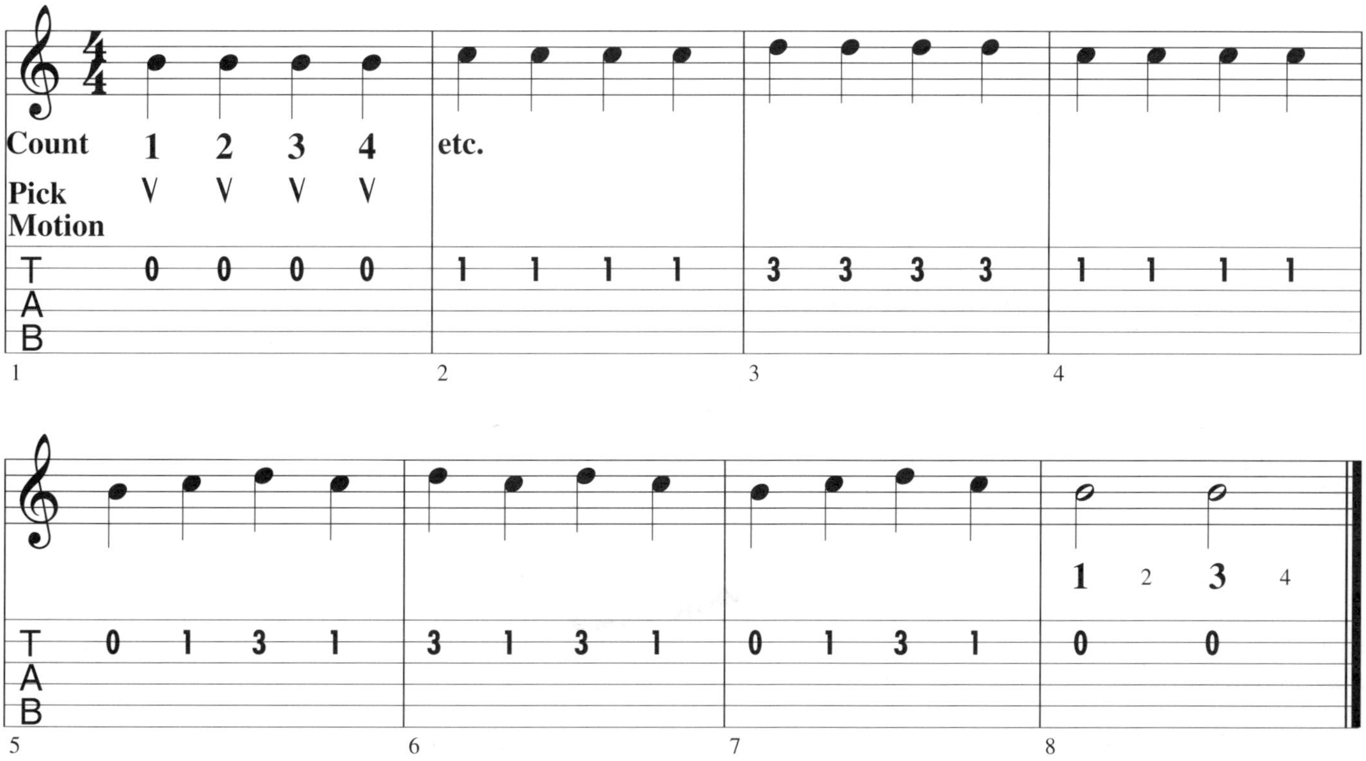
Count 1 2 3 4 etc.
Pick Motion V V V V
T
A
B
0 0 0 0 | 1 1 1 1 | 3 3 3 3 | 1 1 1 1
1 2 3 4
1 2 3 4
0 1 3 1 | 3 1 3 1 | 0 1 3 1 | 0 0
5 6 7 8

## TROUBLESHOOTING

*   Make sure your guitar is in tune (**see Appendix One**).
*   **Watch the music**, not your fingers.
*   Concentrate on learning the notes, rather than memorising the song. To do this, you should play very slowly, naming each note as you play it.
*   Remember to use the correct fingering: **first** finger for **first** fret notes, and **third** finger for **third** fret notes.

The following songs make use of all six notes which you have so far studied.

**11    Song Of Joy (Part One)**

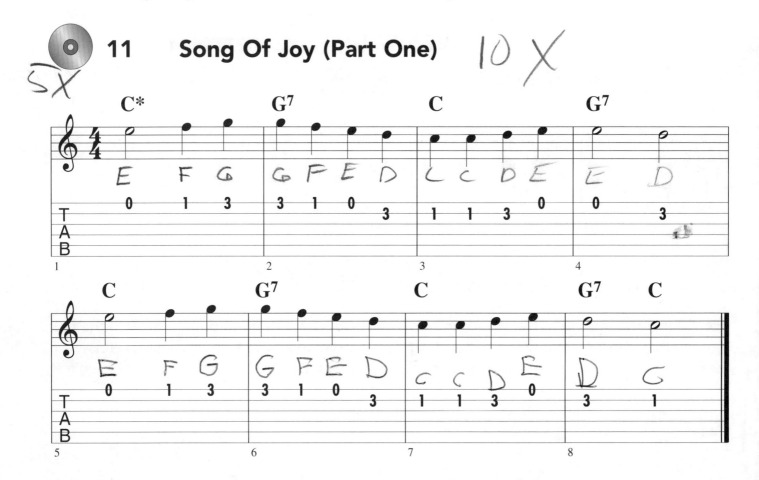

\* **Chord symbols** have been included for students who have some chord knowledge. If you have never played chords, see **Progressive Guitar Method: RHYTHM** by Gary Turner.

**12    Skip To My Lou**

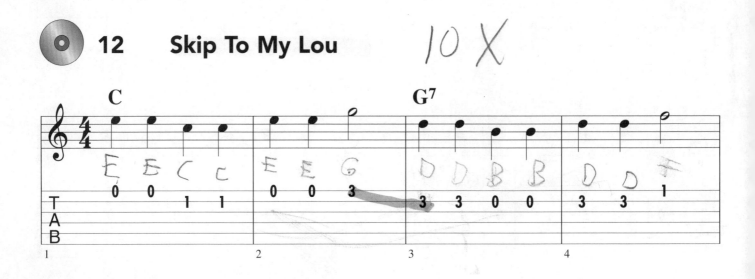

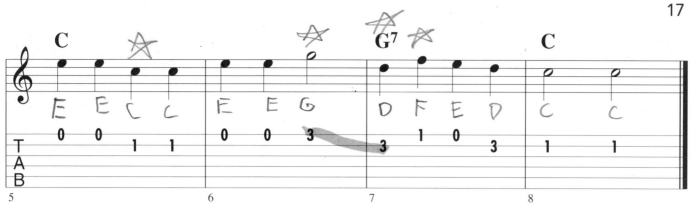

**2 String Blues** introduces the **whole note (or semibreve)** o ,in bars 12 and 13, which is worth four counts. It is played on the first beat, and held for the remaining three, as indicated by the count.

### 13     2 String Blues

*You can now play the songs on pages 8 to 10 of **Guitar Method Book 1: Supplement**.*

# LESSON THREE

## THIRD STRING NOTES

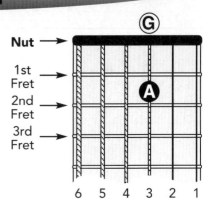

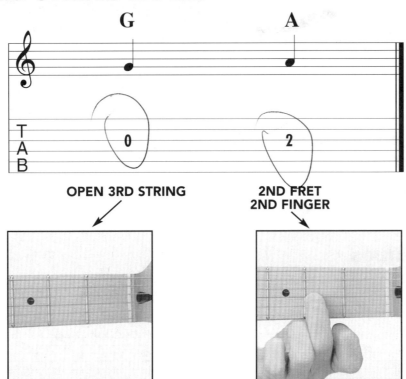

**OPEN 3RD STRING**

**2ND FRET 2ND FINGER**

You now have two **G** notes; the one above and the one at the third fret on the first string. This type of repetition occurs with all notes, since the musical alphabet goes from **A** to **G**, and then back to **A** again. The distance between the two **G** notes is called **octave**.

**14**

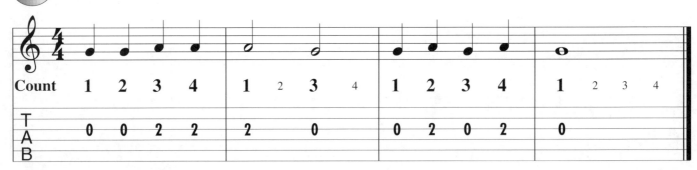

## NOTE SUMMARY

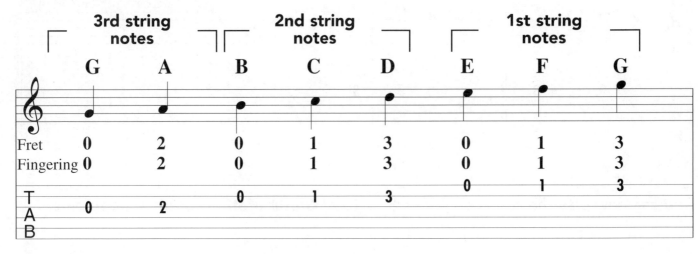

**15** **Aura Lee** X/0

Aura Lee introduces the **music repeat sign** (**Bar 4**), which consists of a thick and thin line, with two dots placed before them. It indicates a repeat of the section of music which has just been played. The repeat sign in the final bar indicates that the song must be repeated from the beginning.

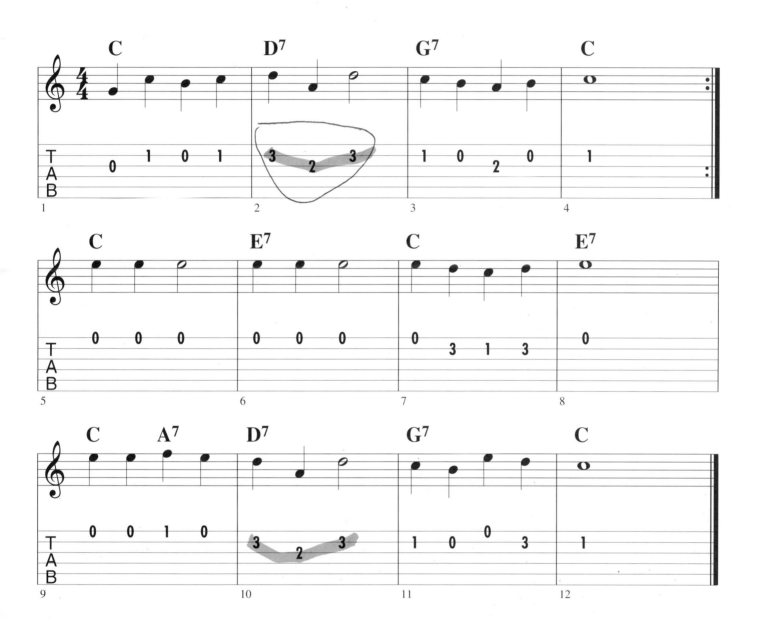

20

## 18    12 Bar Blues

## 19    Michael Row The Boat Ashore

This song introduces **lead-in notes**, which are notes occurring before the first complete bar of music. These notes should be played on counts three and four of a count-in (as indicated). You will notice that the final bar of the song contains only one half note (two counts), which acts as a 'balance' to the lead-in notes. This is quite common, but does not always occur. Lead-in notes are sometimes called pick up notes.

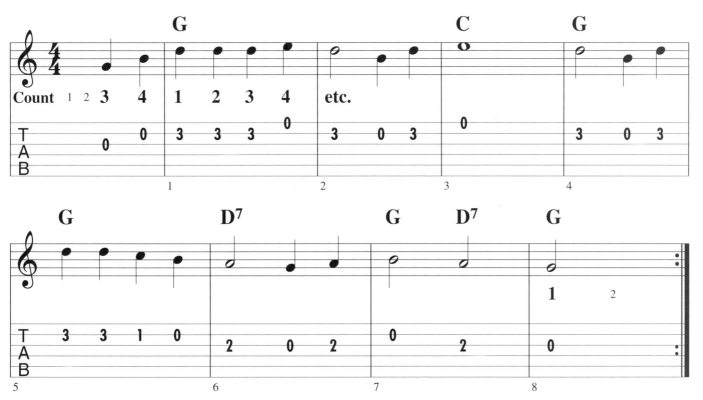

*You can now play the songs on pages 11 and 12 of **Guitar Method Book 1: Supplement**.*

# LESSON FOUR

## FOURTH STRING NOTES

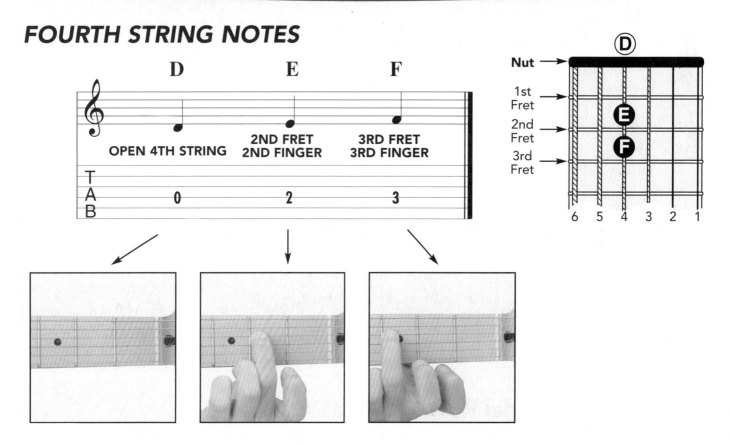

**Ex. 17** is in $\frac{3}{4}$ time, where there are 3 quarter note beats per bar (**see page 11**).

It also introduces the **dotted half note** 𝅗𝅥. which is worth three counts. When a dot is placed after a note it increases the value of that note by a half (**see page 10**).

 **20**

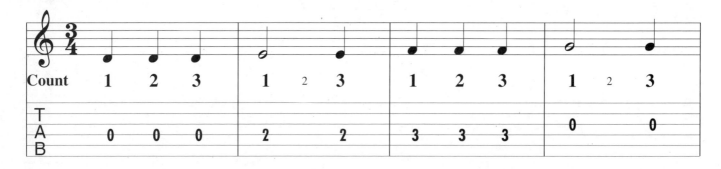

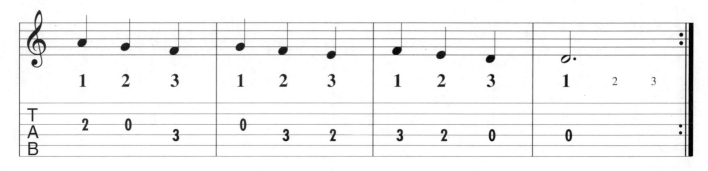

## 21 Molly Malone

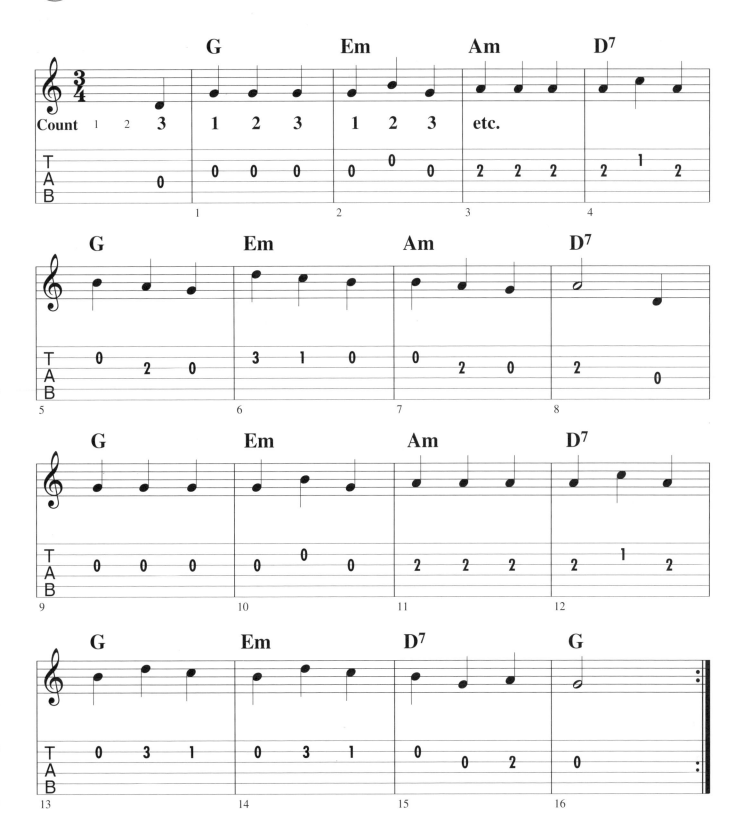

## 22    Will The Circle Be Unbroken

A **tie** is a curved line joining two or more notes of the same pitch. The second note (or notes) is **not played**, but its time value is added to that of the first note. In bar 1 the **G** note is held for a total of 4 counts (2+2) and bar 15 it is held for 6 counts (4+2).

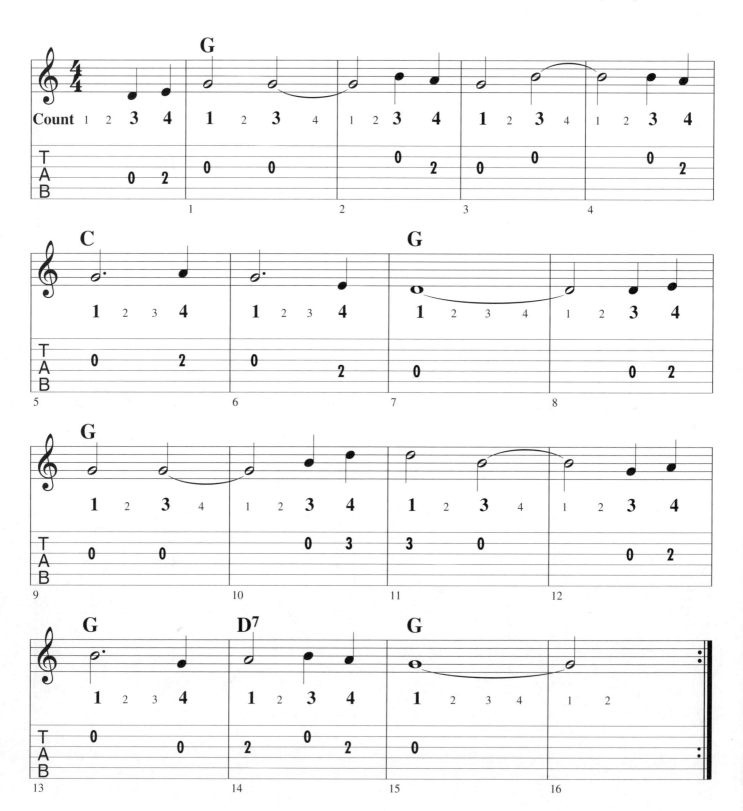

 **23** **Walkin' Blues**

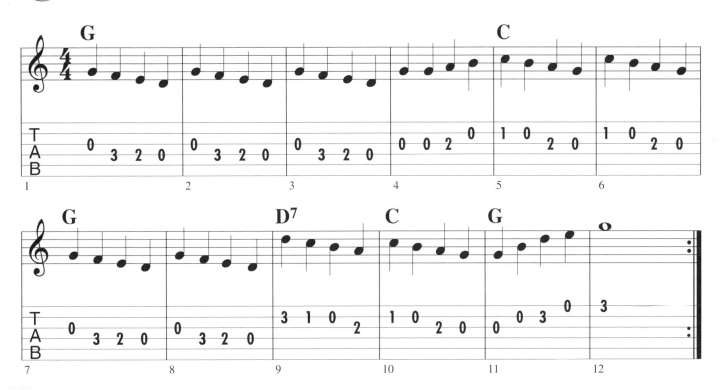

## NOTE SUMMARY

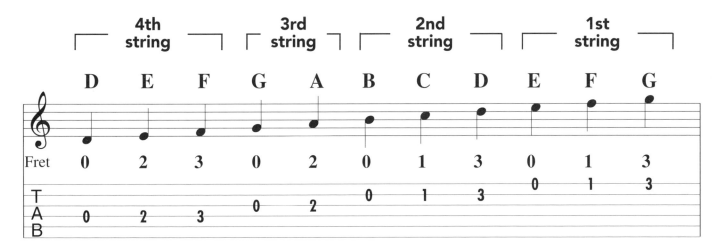

## TROUBLESHOOTING

* Remember to maintain correct left and right hand playing positions (**see photos on page 9**).
* **Count** as you play, and be particularly careful of dotted notes and ties. You may also find it advantageous to tap your foot with the beat.
* Hold the pick correctly, between the thumb and index finger (**see page 8**).
* Be sure to support your wrist and use correct pick technique (**see page 14**).

*You can now play songs on page 13 and 14 of **Guitar Method Book 1: Supplement**.*

# LESSON FIVE

## FIFTH STRING NOTES

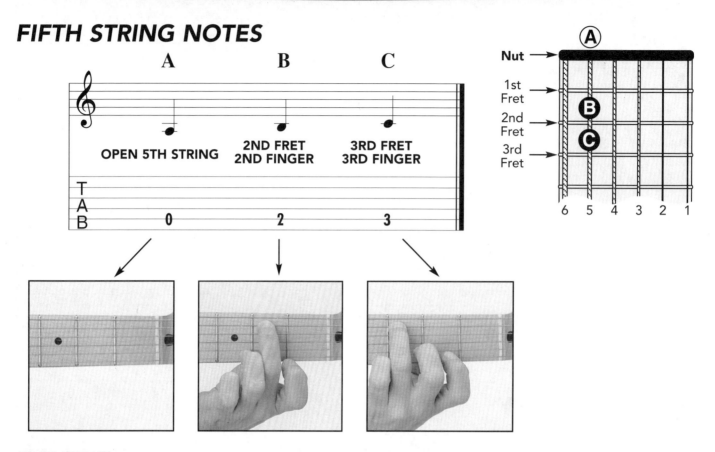

## RESTS

In music, rests are used to indicate periods of silence. For each note value there is a corresponding rest, as outlined in the following table.

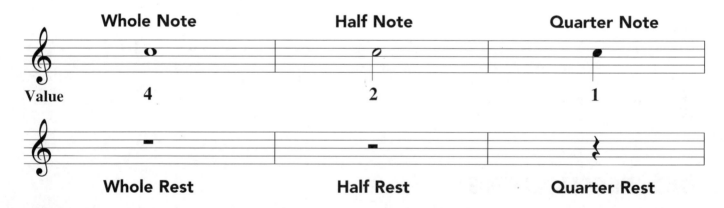

**24** The **C** at the beginning of this exercise stands for **common time**, which is another name for $\frac{4}{4}$ time.

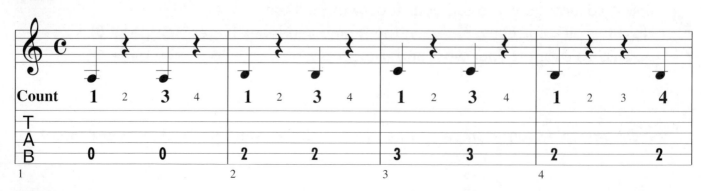

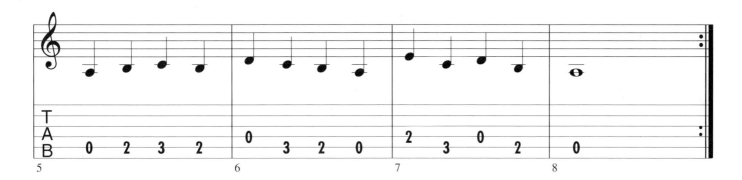

## 25  Banks Of The Ohio

## 26    Blow The Man Down

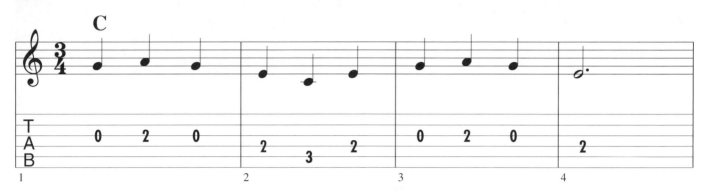

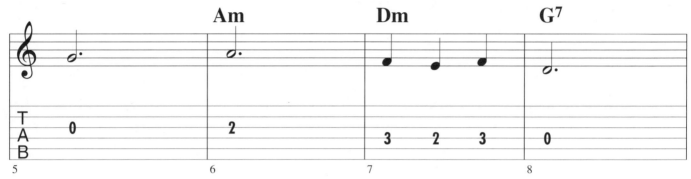

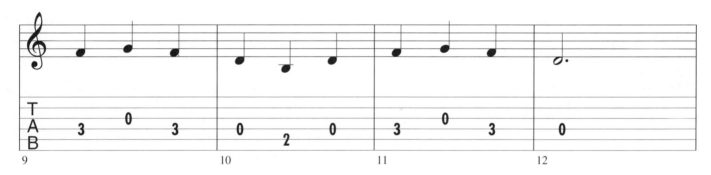

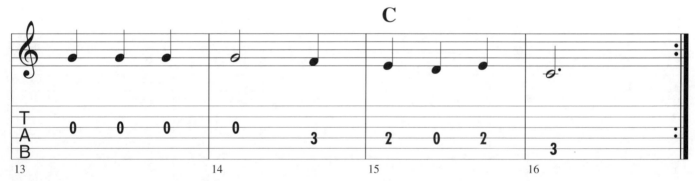

## 27    Volga Boatman

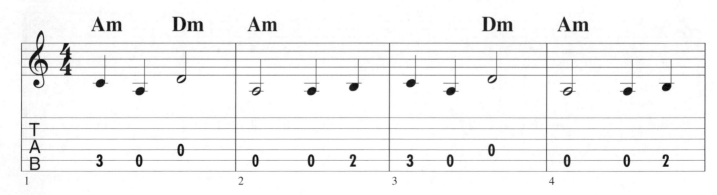

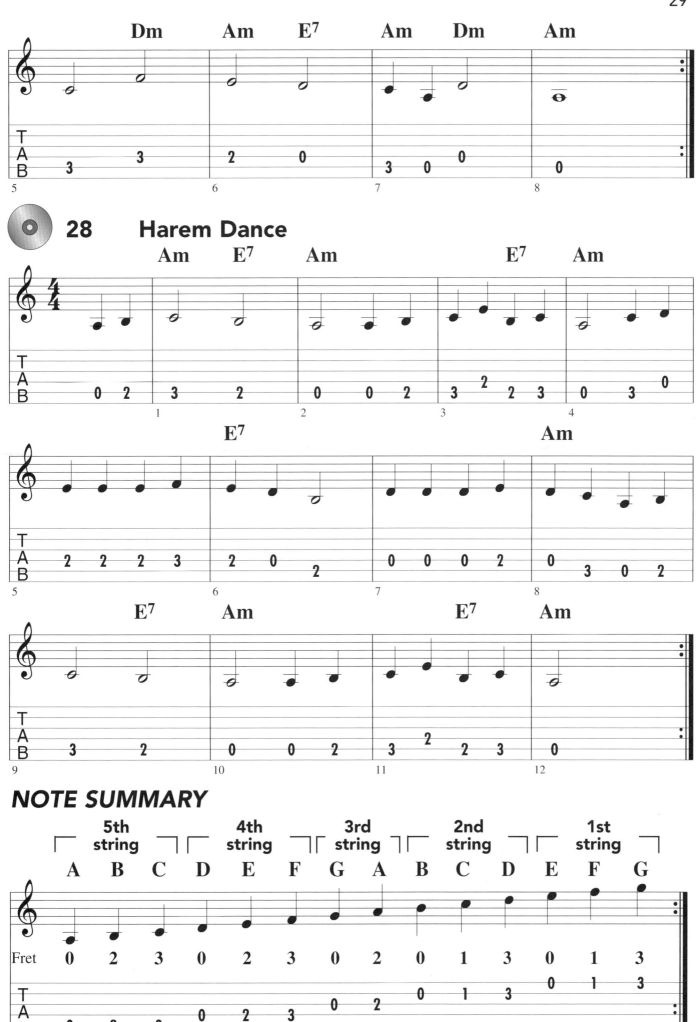

## NOTE SUMMARY

You can now play songs on pages 14 to 17 of *Guitar Method Book 1: Supplement*.

# LESSON SIX

## SIXTH STRING NOTES

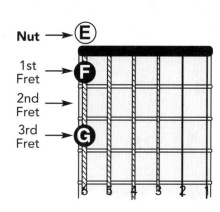

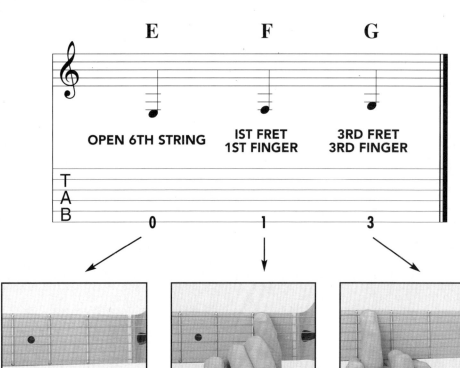

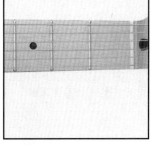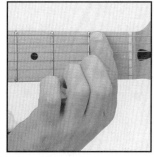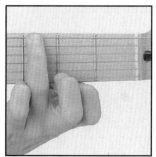

 **29**

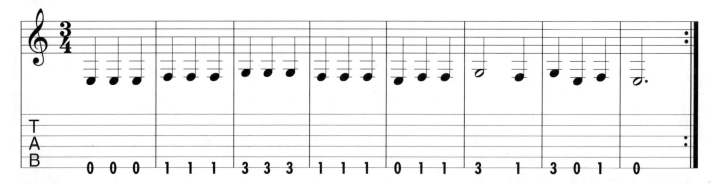

 **30   I Gave My Love A Cherry**

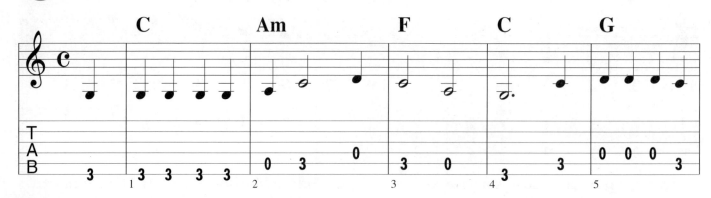

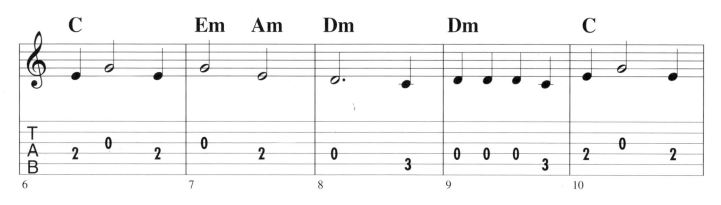

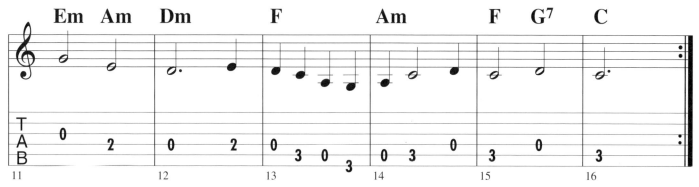

31    **12 Bar Blues In the Key of C**

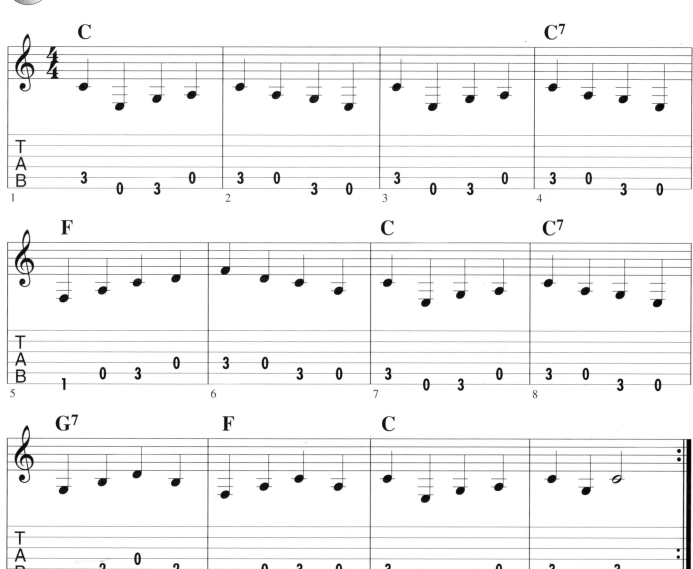

**32 Asturias**

*You can now play songs on pages 18 to 20 of **Guitar Method Book 1: Supplement.***

# OPEN POSITION NOTES

All of the notes you have studied, as summarised below, are in the **open position**. The open position consists of the open string notes and the notes on the first three frets.

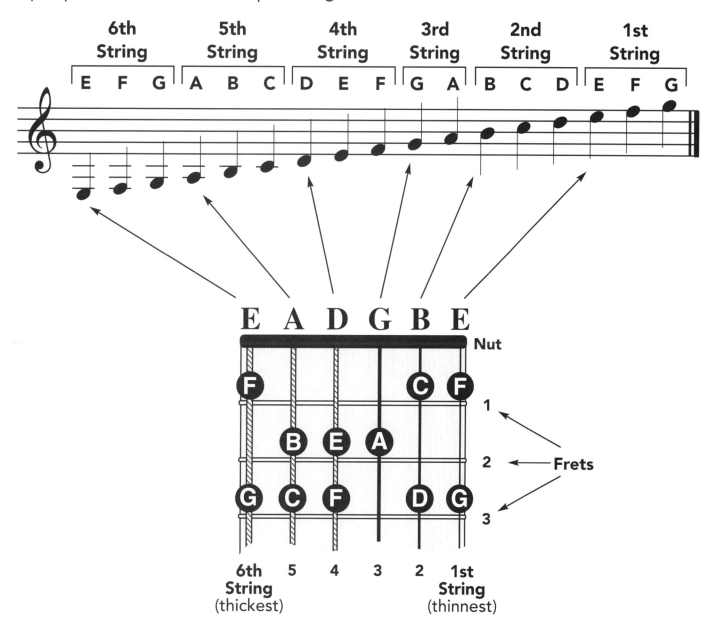

By playing through the notes you will notice **B** to **C** and **E** to **F** are only one fret apart (called a **semitone**), whereas all other notes are two frets apart (called a **tone**). The distance between notes of the musical alphabet can be set out as such:

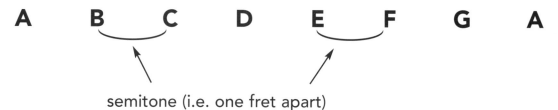

semitone (i.e. one fret apart)

It is essential for you to remember this pattern of notes.

## TROUBLESHOOTING

- Revise all songs and exercises so far studied.
- Double-check your timing and smoothness of sound. To do this, try recording yourself.
- Remember to watch the music, **not** the guitar.

# LESSON SEVEN

## EIGHTH NOTES

An **eighth note (or quaver)** ♪ is worth half a count. Two eighth notes, which are usually joined by a line (called a beam) ♫ , have the same value as a quarter note.

Eighth notes are counted as such:

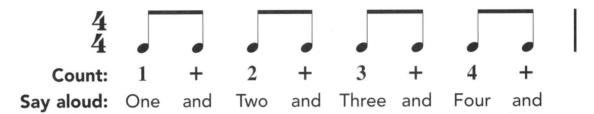

| Count: | 1 | + | 2 | + | 3 | + | 4 | + |
|---|---|---|---|---|---|---|---|---|
| Say aloud: | One | and | Two | and | Three | and | Four | and |

Here is a combination of half notes, quarter notes and eighth notes in $\frac{4}{4}$ time.

| Count: | 1 | 2 | + | 3 | 4 | + | 1 | 2 | 3 | + | 4 | + | 1 | 2 | 3 | 4 | + |
|---|---|---|---|---|---|---|---|---|---|---|---|---|---|---|---|---|---|

The **eighth note rest** ♪, is worth half a count of silence.

## ALTERNATIVE PICKING

All of the songs you have so far played involved a downward pick motion, indicated by V. With the introduction of eighth notes, the technique of down and up ( Λ ) picking is used. This is called **alternate picking**, and it is essential for the development of speed and accuracy.

In alternate picking, use a down pick **on** the beat (the number count) and an up pick **off** the beat (the 'and' count). Try the following exercise:

 **33**

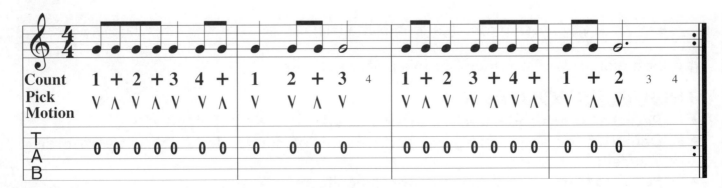

| Count | 1 + 2 + 3 4 + | 1 2 + 3 4 | 1 + 2 3 + 4 + | 1 + 2 3 4 |
|---|---|---|---|---|
| Pick Motion | V Λ V Λ V V Λ | V V Λ V | V Λ V V Λ V Λ | V Λ V |

**34** **12 Bar Blues In the Key of C**

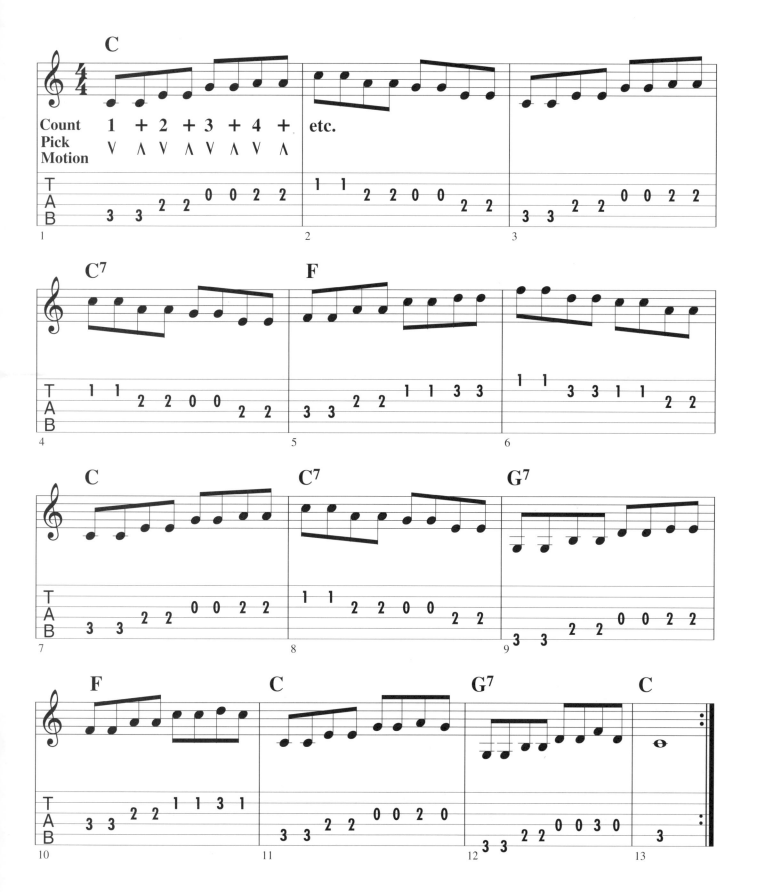

## 35 Waltzing Matilda

# DUETS

It is important for you to be able to play with other musicians and the best practice for this is the study of duets. Duets are written as two independent parts of music, which are indicated by the Roman Numerals at the beginning of each line.
To get the most benefit from duets practice **both** parts.

Playing duets will present specific problems. Be careful of the followng:
*   Make sure to stay on your correct part (e.g. the top or bottom line).
*   Pay particular attention to your timing and try not to stop if the other guitarist makes a mistake.
*   Do not be distracted by the other guitarist's part.

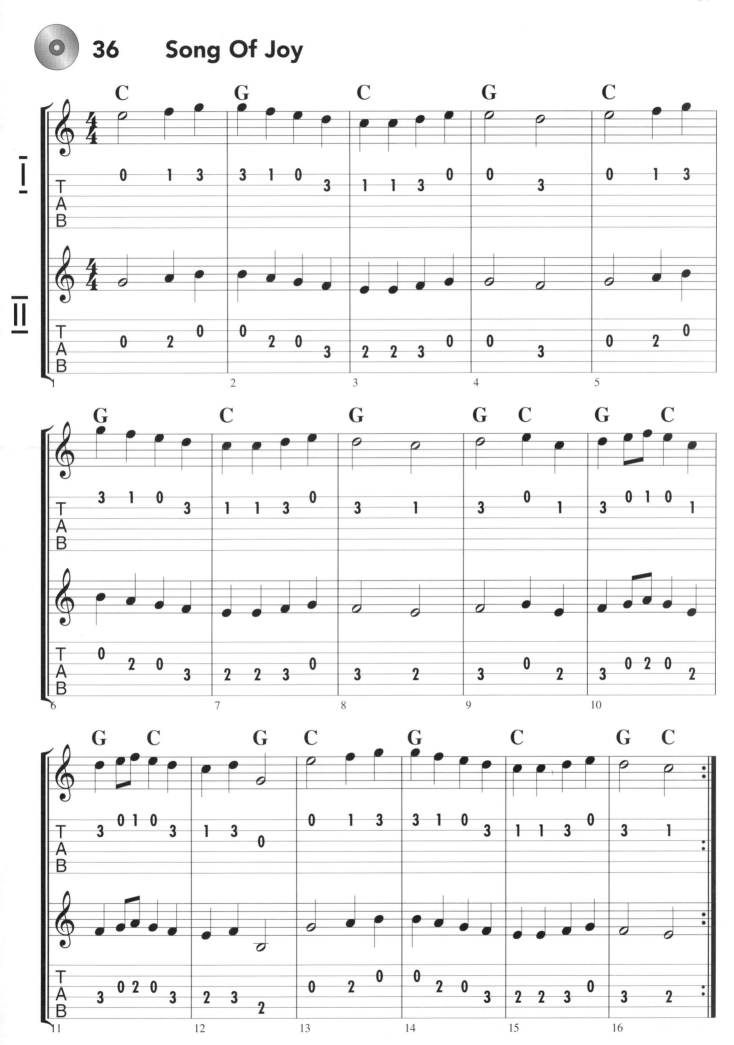

*You can now play songs on pages 20 to 24 of **Guitar Method Book 1: Supplement**.*

# LESSON EIGHT

## SHARPS

A sharp ( ♯ ) is a sign, placed immediately **before** a note, which raises the pitch of that note by **one semitone (one fret)**. When you see a note with a sharp sign in front of it, you should first think of where the normal note is located (in music this is called the **natural note**), and then sharpen it by placing your **next finger** on the **next fret** along. Here are some examples:

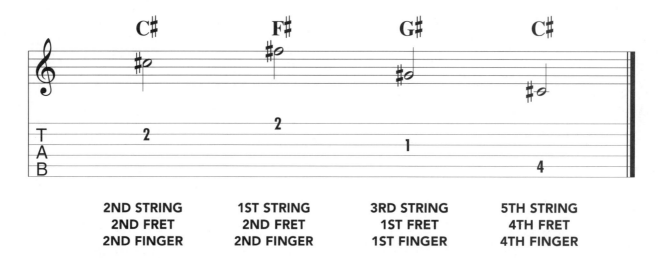

| 2ND STRING | 1ST STRING | 3RD STRING | 5TH STRING |
|---|---|---|---|
| 2ND FRET | 2ND FRET | 1ST FRET | 4TH FRET |
| 2ND FINGER | 2ND FINGER | 1ST FINGER | 4TH FINGER |

The use of the sharp sign introduces five new notes, occurring in between the seven natural notes which you already know. The following exercise outlines all twelve notes which occur within one octave of music. Play through it **very slowly**, and be sure to use correct fingering for the sharpened notes.

 **37**

You will notice that there is no sharp between **B** and **C**, or between **E** and **F**.

The exercise you have just played is called a **chromatic scale**. It is referred to as the **A chromatic scale** because the starting and finishing notes are **A** (this is called the **Key note** or **tonic**). The chromatic scale consists entirely of **semitones** i.e. it moves up (or down) one fret at a time.

**38** Here is the **G** chromatic scale:

When a note is sharpened it **REMAINS** sharp until either a **BAR LINE** or a **NATURAL SIGN** (♮) cancels it. Check the following notes:

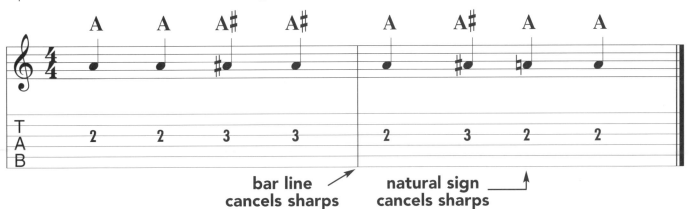

**39** # House Of The Rising Sun

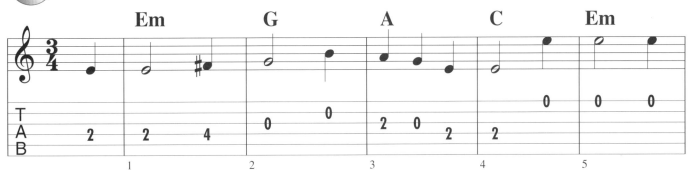

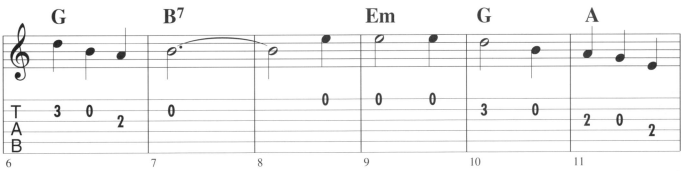

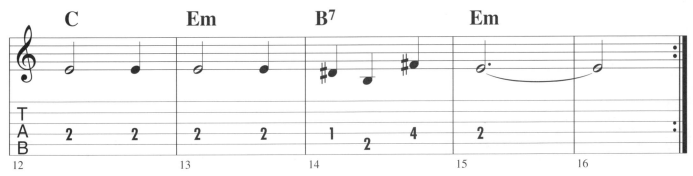

40

Watch your timing with the ties in this song.

**40** **Dark Eyes**

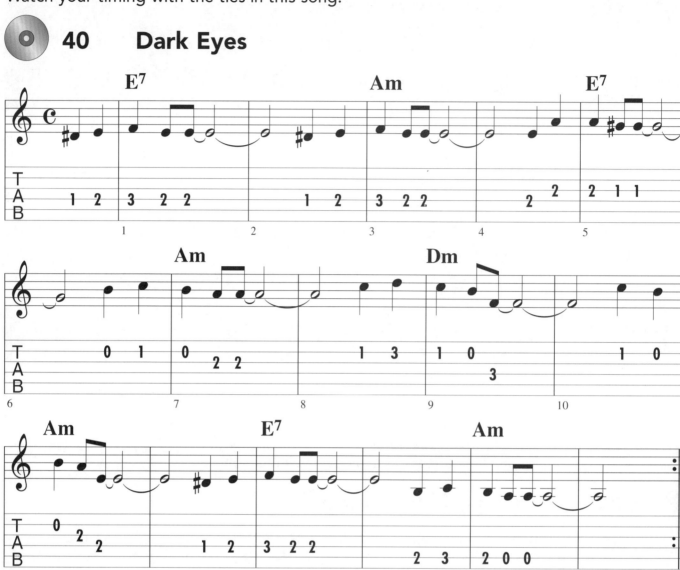

**41** **Minuet**

J.S. Bach

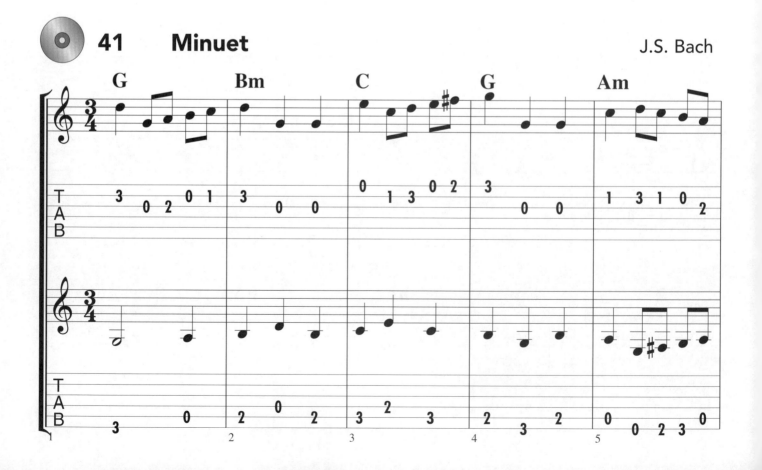

## TROUBLESHOOTING

• Be sure to use the correct fingering for all notes:

  1st fret . . . . .1st finger
  2nd fret . . . .2nd finger
  3rd fret . . . . .3rd finger
  4th fret . . . . .4th finger

• Keep your left hand fingers as close to the strings as possible. This will greatly improve your accuracy and speed.

• **Watch** the music and **read** the notes. Occasionally you should just name the notes in a song, without actually playing through it.

*You can now play songs on pages 25 to 29 of* **Guitar Method Book 1: Supplement.**

# LESSON NINE

## FLATS

A **flat** (♭) is a sign, placed immediately **before** a note, which **lowers** the pitch of that note by one semitone. Locate the following flats:

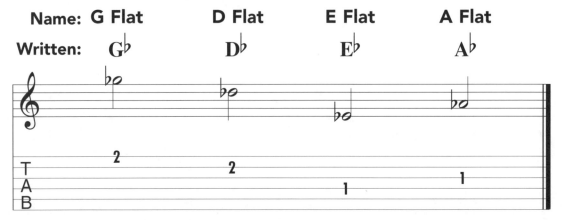

When an open string note is flattened, the new note must be located on the **next lower string** e.g.:

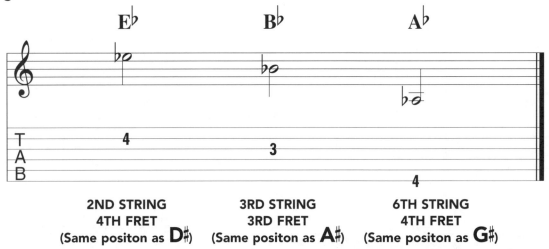

| 2ND STRING | 3RD STRING | 6TH STRING |
|---|---|---|
| 4TH FRET | 3RD FRET | 4TH FRET |
| (Same positon as **D♯**) | (Same positon as **A♯**) | (Same positon as **G♯**) |

You will notice that it is possible for the same note (in pitch) to have two different names. For example, F♯ = G♭ and G♯ = A♭. These are referred to as **enharmonic** notes. The following fretboard diagram outlines all of the notes in the **first position** on the guitar (including both names for the enharmonic notes). The first position consists of the open string notes and the notes on the first four frets.

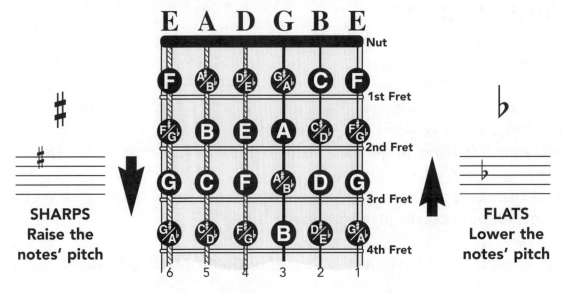

Here are two octaves of the **E chromatic scale**, ascending using sharps and descending using flats.

As with sharps, flats are cancelled by a bar line or by a natural sign.

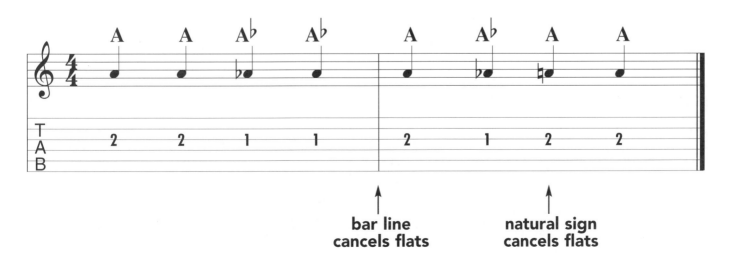

**43**     **8 Bar Blues**

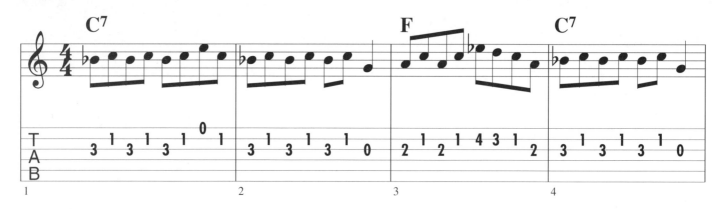

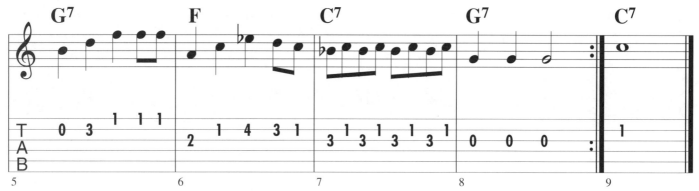

 **44**     **Hall of the Mountain King**

This song introduces **first** and **second endings** (**see Line 6**). On the first time through, ending **one** is played, as indicated by the bracket:     | **1.**
The section of music is then repeated (go back to the beginning of line 5) and on the second time ending **two** is played. Be careful **not** to play both endings together.

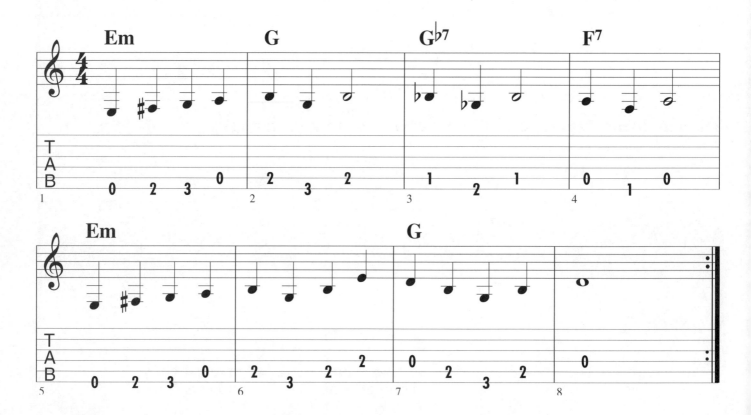

If you are playing the chords to this song it is easier to play the G♭7, F7 and B chords as **bar chords**. To learn how to play bar chords see *Progressive Guitar Method: Bar Chords.*

46

**45**   **Blues Traveller**

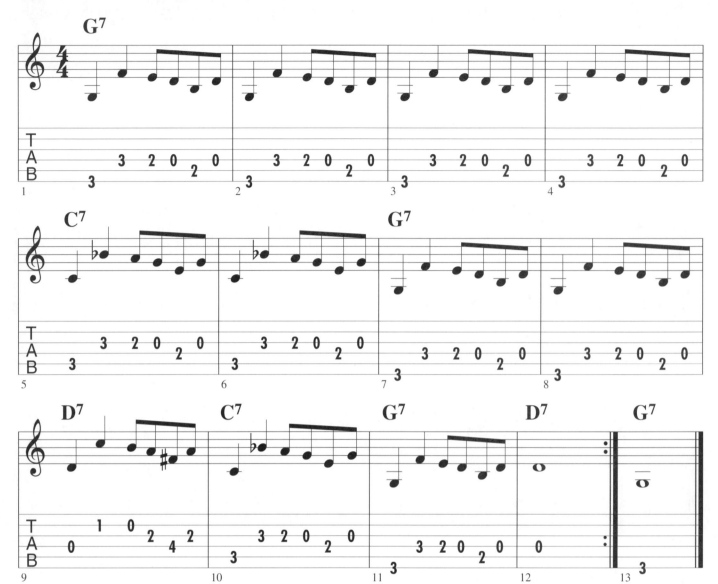

**46**   **Blue Seas**

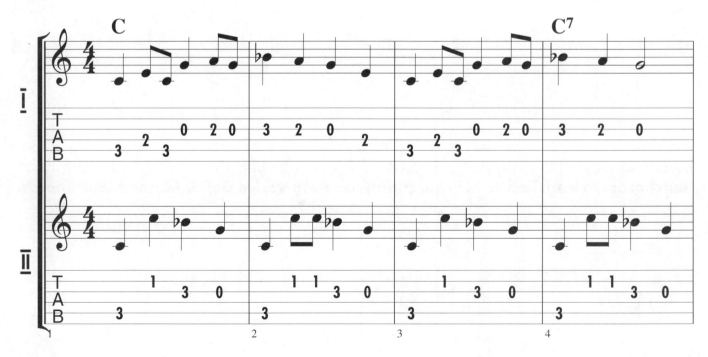

You can now play the songs on pages 30 to 32 of **Guitar Method Book 1: Supplement.**

# LESSON TEN
# DOTTED QUARTER NOTES

The **dotted quarter note** is worth 1½ counts. It has the same time value as a quarter note tied to an eighth note, i.e.

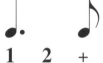

When a dotted quarter note is followed by an eighth note, as in Greensleeves, the count is as follows:

1 2 +

 **47** **Greensleeves**

This song features some difficult left hand fingering passages which will require special attention. In any music you play, be sure to **isolate** difficult sections and practice them thoroughly.
The eighth notes in Greensleeves are played with an up pick, as indicated.

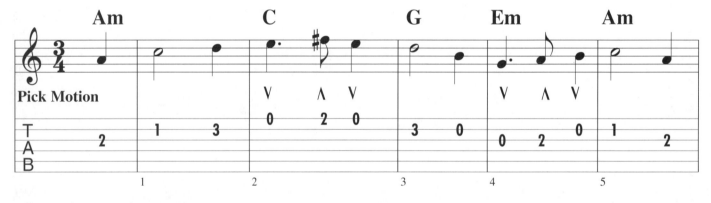

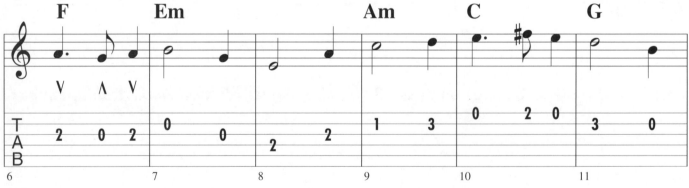

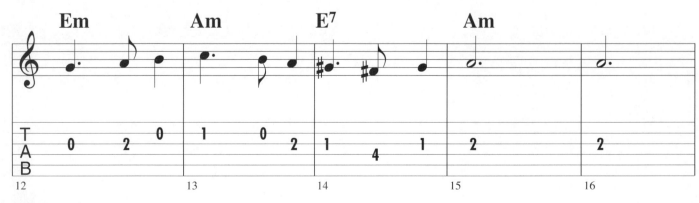

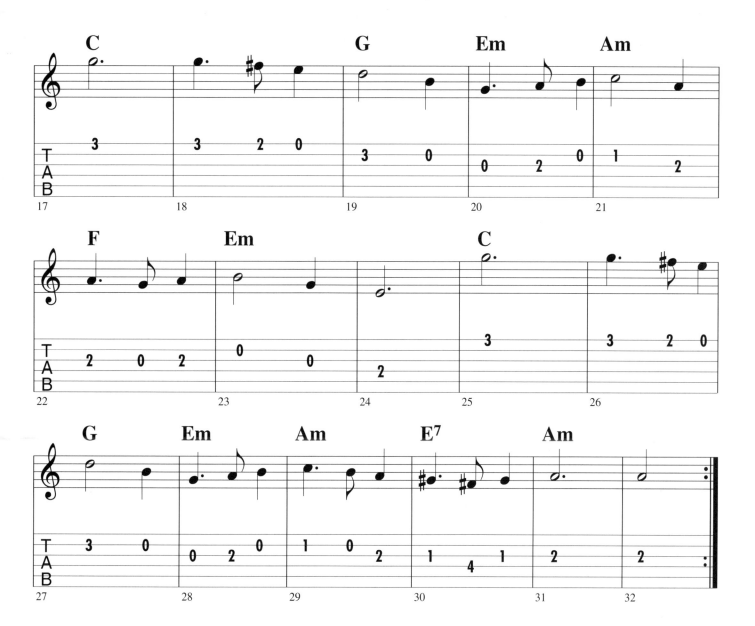

# THE 'HIGH' A NOTE

The **'high' A note** is located on the 5th fret of the first string, and is played using the **fourth** finger.

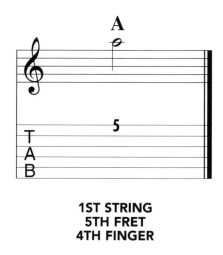

**1ST STRING
5TH FRET
4TH FINGER**

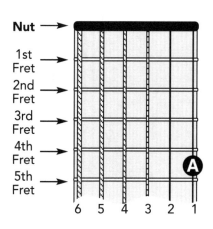

Practice the following exercise slowly and carefully. Watch the music!

 **48**

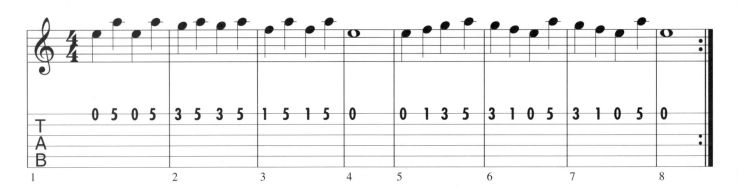

 **49** **Scarborough Fair**

Scarborough Fair uses the high A note in bars 6, 8 and 9. The abbreviation **rit**, in bar 15, stands for **ritardando**, which means to **gradually slow down**.

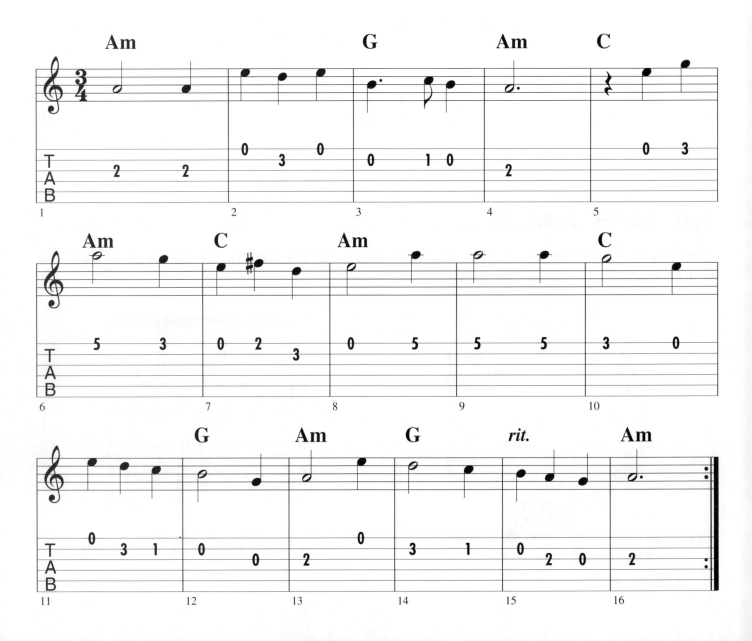

## 50  Auld Lang Syne

## TROUBLESHOOTING

- Revise all pieces so far studied. This revision should become the 'warm up' of your practice sessions.
- Keep your left hand fingers as close as possible to the strings. They should 'hover' no more than a half inch (1cm) above the strings.
- **Always** play with a pick.

*You can now play the songs on pages 33 to 37 of* **Guitar Method Book 1: Supplement.**

# SUPPLEMENTARY PIECES

Here are some graded songs for extra study.

 **51**    **God Rest Ye Merry Gentlemen**

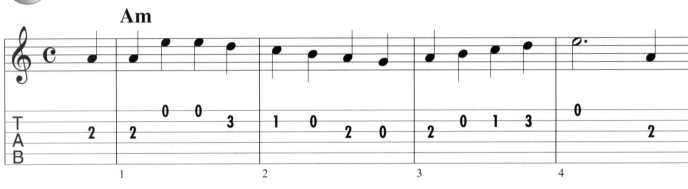

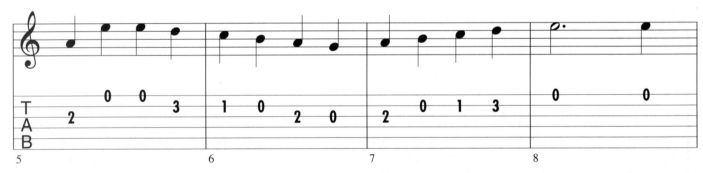

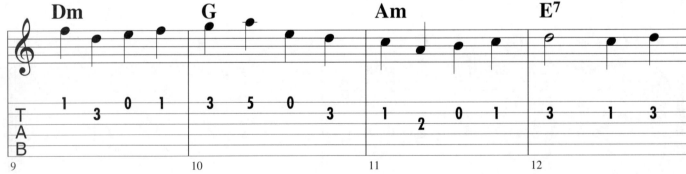

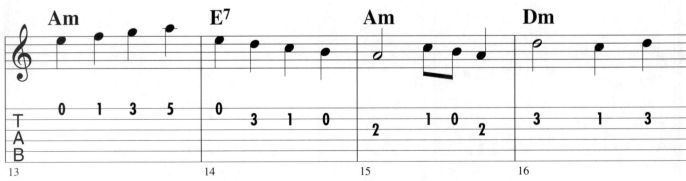

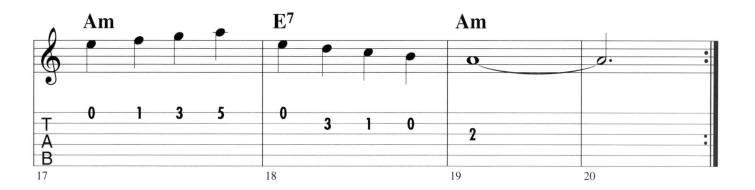

## 52    Rick's Blues

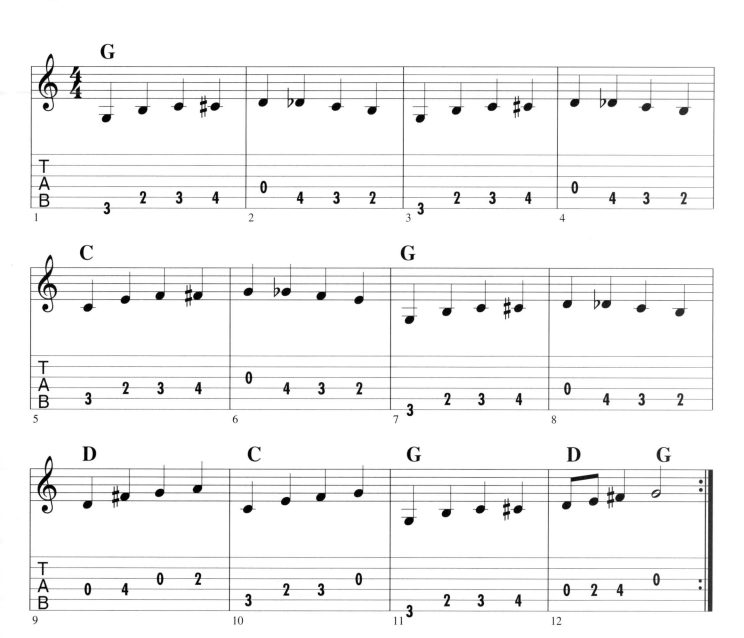

54

**53    The Star Spangled Banner**

**54** **Silent Night**

**55**    **When The Saints Go Marching In**

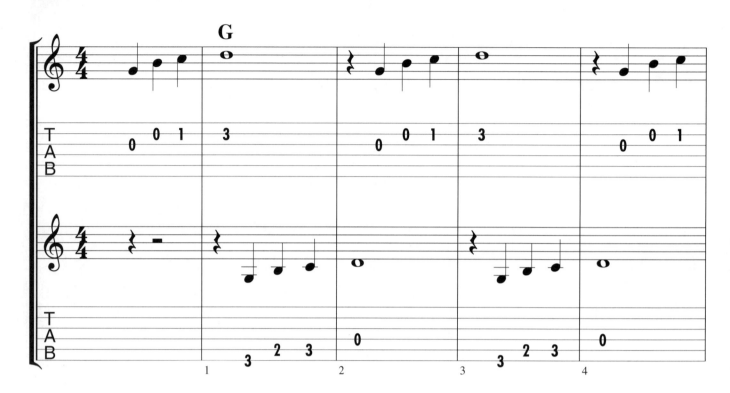

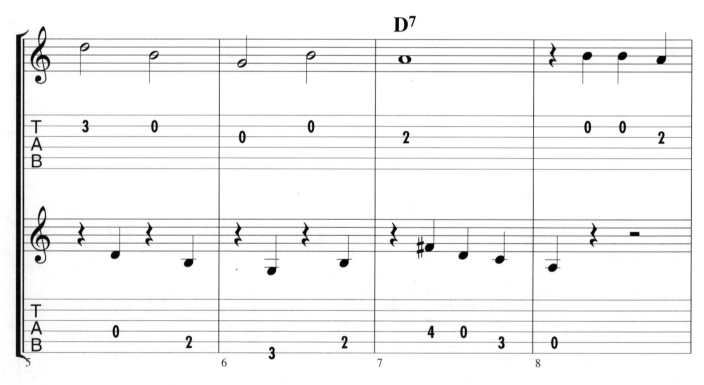

**Over 70 more supplementary pieces can be found in**
## Progressive Guitar Method Book 1: Supplement.
**This book also contains 8 more lessons which introduce;**
**Major scales, Keys, Triplets, $\frac{6}{8}$ time, Sixteenth notes, Syncopation and Swing.**

# APPENDIX ONE – TUNING

It is essential for your guitar to be in tune, so that the notes you play will sound correct. The main problem with tuning for most students is that the ear is not able to determine slight differences in pitch. For this reason you should seek the aid of a teacher or an experienced guitarist.

Several methods can be used to tune the guitar. These include:
1. Tuning to another musical instrument (e.g. a piano, or another guitar).
2. Tuning to pitch pipes or a tuning fork.
3. Tuning with an electronic tuner.
4. Tuning the guitar to itself.

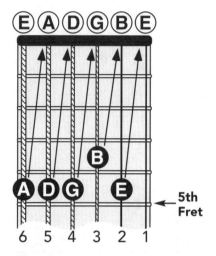

The most common and useful of these is the latter; tuning the guitar to itself. This method involves finding notes of the same pitch on different strings. The diagram outlines the notes used:

The method of tuning is as follows:
**1.** Tune the open 6th string to either:
   (a) The open 6th string of another guitar.
   (b) A piano.

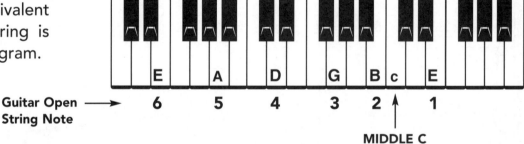

The piano note equivalent of the open 6th string is indicated on the diagram.

(c) **Pitch pipes** which produce notes that correspond with each of the 6 open strings.

(d) **A tuning fork**. Most tuning forks give the note A.

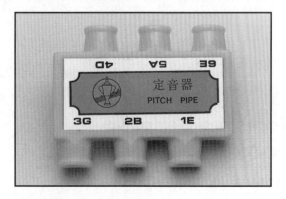

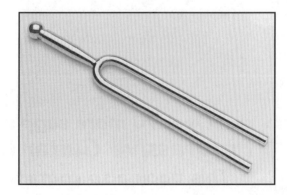

To produce sound from the tuning fork, hold it by the stem and tap one of the prongs against something hard. This will set up a vibration, which can be heard clearly when the bass of the stem is then placed on a solid surface, e.g. a guitar body.

2. Place a finger on the 6th string at the 5th fret. Now play the open **A** (5th string). If the guitar is to be in tune, then these two notes must have the same pitch (i.e. sound the same). If they do not sound the same, the 5th string must be adjusted to match the note produced on the 6th string. Thus the 5th string is tuned in relation to the 6th string.

3. Tune the open 4th string to the note on the 5th fret of the 5th string, using the method outlined above.

4. Tune all other strings using the same procedure, remembering that the open **B** string (2nd) is tuned to the 4th fret (check diagram) while all other strings are tuned to the 5th fret.

5. Strum an open **E** major chord, (**see page 47**) to check if your guitar is tuned correctly. At first you may have some difficulty deciding whether or not the chord sound is correct, but as your ear improves you will become more familiar with the correct sound of the chord.

Tuning may take you many months to master, and you should practice it constantly. The guidance of a teacher will be an invaluable aid in the early stages of guitar tuning.

## *TUNING HINTS*

One of the easiest ways to practice tuning is to actually start with the guitar in tune and then de-tune one string. When you do this, always take the string down in pitch (i.e. loosen it) as it is easier to tune 'up' to a given note rather than 'down' to it. As an example, de-tune the 4th string (**D**). If you play a melody now, the guitar will sound out of tune, even though only one string has been altered (so remember that if you guitar is out of tune it may only be one string at fault).

Following the correct method, you must tune the 4th string against the **D** note at the 5th fret of the 5th string. Play the note loudly, and listen carefully to the sound produced. This will help you retain the correct pitch in your mind when tuning the next string.

Now that you have listened carefully to the note that you want, the **D** string must be tuned to it. pick the **D** string, and turn its tuning key at the same time, and you will hear the pitch of the string change (it will become higher as the tuning key tightens the string). It is important to follow this procedure, so that you hear the sound of the string at all times, as it tightens. You should also constantly refer back to the correct sound that is required (i.e. the **D** note on the 5th fret of the 5th string).

## *ELECTRONIC TUNERS*

Electronic Tuners make tuning your guitar very easy. They indicate the exact pitch of each string. It is still recommended however, that you practice tuning your guitar by the above method to help improve your musicianship.

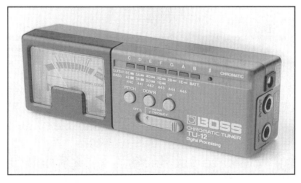

*Electronic Guitar Tuner*

# APPENDIX TWO – CHORD CHART

All the chords used throughout this book can be found in the chord chart below. For a complete knowledge of chords and rhythm techniques see **Progressive Guitar Method: Rhythm** and **Progressive Guitar Method: Chords** by Gary Turner.

## MAJOR CHORDS

*Chord Symbol*

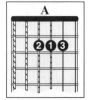 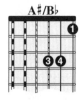 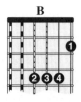 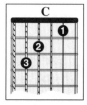  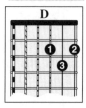

 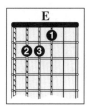 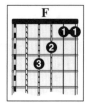  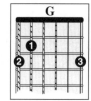 

## MINOR CHORDS

*Chord Symbol* **m**

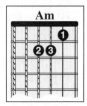 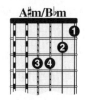 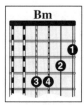   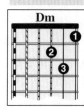

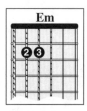    

## SEVENTH CHORDS

*Chord Symbol* **7**

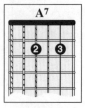 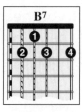   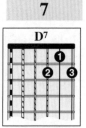

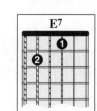   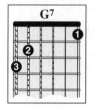 

**1** indicate 1st finger    **3** indicates 3rd finger    A broken line indicates that a string is not to be played.

**2** indicates 2nd finger    **4** indicates 4th finger

# GLOSSARY OF MUSICAL TERMS

**Accidental** — a sign used to show a temporary change in pitch of a note (i.e. sharp ♯, flat ♭, double sharp 𝄪, double flat ♭♭, or natural ♮). The sharps or flats in a key signature are not regarded as accidentals.

**Ad lib** — to be played at the performer's own discretion.

**Allegretto** — moderately fast.

**Allegro** — fast and lively.

**Anacrusis** — a note or notes occurring before the first bar of music (also called 'lead-in' notes).

**Andante** — an easy walking pace.

**Arpeggio** — the playing of a chord in single note fashion.

**Bar** — a division of music occurring between two bar lines (also called a 'measure').

**Bar chord** — a chord played with one finger lying across all six strings.

**Bar line** — a vertical line drawn across the staff which divides the music into equal sections called bars.

**Bass** — the lower regions of pitch in general. On guitar, the 4th, 5th and 6th strings.

**Capo** — a device placed across the neck of a guitar to allow a key change without alteration of the chord shapes.

**Chord** — a combination of three or more different notes played together.

**Chord progression** — a series of chords played as a musical unit (e.g. as in a song).

**Chromatic scale** — a scale ascending and descending in semitones.

e.g. **C** chromatic scale:

ascending:    C        C♯       D       D♯       E       F       F♯       G       G♯       A       A♯       B       C

descending:  C        B       B♭      A       A♭      G       G♭      F       E       E♭      D       D♭      C

**Clef** — a sign placed at the beginning of each staff of music which fixes the location of a particular note on the staff, and hence the location of all other notes, e.g.

Treble Staff                               Bass Staff

**Coda** — an ending section of music, signified by the sign ⊕ .

**Common time** — and indication of ⁴⁄₄ time — four quarter note beats per bar (also indicated by 𝄴 )

**D.C al fine** — a repeat from the beginning to the word 'fine'.

**Dot** — a sign placed after a note indicating that its time value is extended by a half. e.g.

♩ = 2 counts    ♩. = 3 counts

**Duration** — the time value of each note.

**Dynamics** — the varying degrees of softness (indicated by the term 'piano') and loudness (indicated by the term 'forte') in music.

**Eighth note** — a note with the value of half a beat in ⁴⁄₄ time, indicated thus ♪ (also called a quaver).

**The eighth note rest** — indicating half a beat of silence, is written: 𝄾

**Enharmonic** — describes the difference in notation, but not in pitch, of two notes: e.g.

F♯ or G♭

**Fermata** — a sign, 𝄐 , used to indicate that a note or chord is held to the player's own discretion (also called a 'pause sign').

**First and second endings** — signs used where two different endings occur. On the first time through ending one is played (indicated by the bracket ⌐1⌐ ); then the progression is repeated and ending two is played (indicated ⌐2⌐ ).

**Flat** — a sign, ( ♭ )used to lower the pitch of a note by one semitone.

**Forte** — loud. Indicated by the sign $f$ .

**Half note** — a note with the value of two beats in 𝄴 time, indicated thus: ♩ (also called a minim). The half note rest, indicating two beats of silence, is written: ▬ ◄— third staff line.

**Harmonics** — a chime like sound created by lightly touching a vibrating string at certain points along the fret board.

**Harmony** — the simultaneous sounding of two or more different notes.

**Improvise** — to perform spontaneously; i.e. not from memory or from a written copy.

**Interval** — the distance between any two notes of different pitches.

**Key** — describes the notes used in a composition in regards to the major or minor scale from which they are taken; e.g. a piece 'in the key of C major' describes the melody, chords, etc., as predominantly consisting of the notes, **C, D, E, F, G, A,** and **B** — i.e. from the **C** scale.

**Key signature** — a sign, placed at the beginning of each staff of music, directly after the clef, to indicate the key of a piece. The sign consists of a certain number of sharps or flats, which represent the sharps or flats found in the scale of the piece's key. e.g.

 indicates a scale with **F♯** and **C♯** , which is **D** major; **D E F♯ G A B C♯ D**. Therefore the key is **D** major.

**Lead-In** — same as anacrusis (also called a pick-up).

**Leger lines** — small horizontal lines upon which notes are written when their pitch is either above or below the range of the staff, e.g.

Leger line

**Legato** — smoothly, well connected.

**Lyric** — words that accompany a melody.

**Major scale** — a series of eight notes in alphabetical order based on the interval sequence tone - tone - semitone - tone - tone - tone - semitone, giving the familiar sound **do re mi fa so la ti do**.

**Melody** — a succession of notes of varying pitch and duration, and having a recognizable musical shape.

**Metronome** — a device which indicates the number of beats per minute, and which can be adjusted in accordance to the desired tempo.

e.g. **MM** (Maelzel Metronome)  ♩ = 60 — indicates 60 quarter note beats per minute.

**Moderato** — at a moderate pace.

**Natural** — a sign ( ♮ )used to cancel our the effect of a sharp or flat. The word is also used to describe the notes **A, B, C, D, E, F** and **G**; e.g. 'the natural notes'.

**Notation** — the written representation of music, by means of symbols (music on a staff), letters (as in chord and note names) and diagrams (as in chord illustrations.)

**Note** — a single sound with a given pitch and duration.

**Octave** — the distance between any given note with a set frequency, and another note with exactly double that frequency. Both notes will have the same letter name;

**A 220    A 440**

**Open chord** — a chord that contains at least one open string.

**Pitch** — the sound produced by a note, determined by the frequency of the string vibrations. The pitch relates to a note being referred to as 'high' or 'low'.

**Plectrum** — a small object (often of a triangular shape) made of plastic which is used to pick or strum the strings of a guitar.

**Position** — a term used to describe the location of the left hand on the fret board. The left hand position is determined by the fret location of the first finger, e.g.
The 1st position refers to the 1st to 4th frets. The 3rd position refers to the 3rd to 6th frets and so on.

**Quarter note** — a note with the value of one beat in $\frac{4}{4}$ time, indicated thus ♩ (also called a crotchet). The quarter note rest, indicating one beat of silence, is written: 𝄽 .

**Repeat signs** — in music, used to indicate a repeat of a section of music, by means of two dots placed before a double bar line:

In chord progressions, a repeat sign ✗ , indicates an exact repeat of the previous bar.

**Rhythm** — the note after which a chord or scale is named (also called 'key note').

**Semitone** — the smallest interval used in conventional music. On guitar, it is a distance of one fret.

**Sharp** — a sign ( ♯ ) used to raise the pitch of a note by one semitone.

**Staccato** — to play short and detached. Indicated by a dot placed above the note:

**Staff** — five parallel lines together with four spaces, upon which music is written.

**Syncopation** — the placing of an accent on a normally unaccented beat. e.g.:

**Tablature** — a system of writing music which represents the position of the player's fingers (not the pitch of the notes, but their position on the guitar). A chord diagram is a type of tablature. Notes can also be written using tablature thus:

**Music Notation**     **Tablature**

Each line represents a string, and each number represents a fret.

**Tempo** — the speed of a piece.

**Tie** — a curved line joining two or more notes of the same pitch, where the second note(s) is not played, but its time value is added to that of the first note.

In Example 2, the first note is held for seven counts.

**Timbre** — a quality which distinguishes a note produced on one instrument from the same note produced on any other instrument (also called 'tone colour'). A given note on the guitar will sound different (and therefore distinguishable) from the same pitched note on piano, violin, flute etc. There is usually also a difference in timbre from one guitar to another.

**Time signature** — a sign at the beginning of a piece which indicates, by means of figures, the number of beats per bar (top figure), and the type of note receiving one beat (bottom figure).

**Tone** — a distance of two frets; i.e. the equivalent of two semitones.

**Transposition** — the process of changing music from one key to another.

**Treble** — the upper regions of pitch in general.

**Treble clef** — a sign placed at the beginning of the staff to fix the pitch of the notes placed on it. The treble clef (also called 'G clef') is placed so that the second line indicates as G note:

 ← **G line**

**Wedge mark** — indicates pick direction; e.g: **V** = down pick, **Λ** = up pick

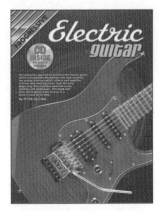

## PROGRESSIVE ELECTRIC GUITAR
### FOR BEGINNING ELECTRIC GUITARISTS
An innovative approach to learning the electric guitar which incorporates the volume and tone controls, the pickup selector switch, the tremolo arm, effects and amplifier settings into learning music from the very beginning. Explains and demonstrates all the essential chords, scales, rhythms and expressive techniques such as slides, bends, trills and vibrato. Also contains lessons on understanding the bass and drums and how to create parts which work with them. This book will have the student ready to play in a band in next to no time.

## PROGRESSIVE BLUES GUITAR
### FOR BEGINNING BLUES GUITARISTS
A great introduction to the world of Blues Guitar. Covers all the essential rhythms used in Blues and R&B along with turnarounds, intros and endings, and gaining control of 12 and 8 bar Blues forms. Also explains and demonstrates the Blues scale, major and minor pentatonic scales and 7th arpeggios in a logical system for playing over the entire fretboard. Contains all the classic Blues sounds such as note bending, slides, and vibrato demonstrated in over 100 licks and solos in a variety of Blues styles.

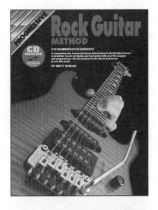

## PROGRESSIVE ROCK GUITAR METHOD
### FOR BEGINNER TO ADVANCED
An easy to follow, lesson by lesson introduction to Rock Guitar. Covers in detail the basics of rhythm and lead guitar with over 50 examples and progressions. Learn to use triplet, syncopated and shuffle rhythms as well as right hand damping and several different right hand strums. Also contains a chord chart for easy reference. You do not need to be able to read music to use this book.

## PROGRESSIVE CLASSICAL GUITAR METHOD
### FOR BEGINNER TO ADVANCED
A comprehensive, lesson by lesson method covering all aspects of basic classical guitar technique such as proper hand techniques, progressing throught the most common keys and incorporating some of the world's most popular classical guitar pieces in solo or duet form. Music theory including the introduction of several different time signatures, open and bar chords and scales are also part of this easy to follow classical guitar method.

## PROGRESSIVE FUNK AND R&B GUITAR METHOD
### FOR BEGINNER TO ADVANCED
This book demonstrates many of the classic Funk sounds, using both rhythm and lead playing, since a good Funk player needs to be equally comfortable with both. A variety of chord forms are introduced within a framework that quickly allows the student to play confidently over the entire fretboard. Features an innovative approach to learning rhythms and applying them to riffs and grooves.